Routledge Revivals

METHODS AND USES OF HYPNOSIS AND SELF-HYPNOSIS

METHODS AND USES
OF
HYPNOSIS & SELF-HYPNOSIS

A TREATISE ON THE POWERS OF THE SUBCONSCIOUS MIND

By

BERNARD HOLLANDER

M.D., M.R.C.S., L.R.C.P.
Corresponding Member of the Royal Academy of Medicine of Madrid

Routledge Revivals
Routledge
Taylor & Francis Group

First published in 1928 by George Allen & Unwin Ltd.

This edition first published in 2018 by Routledge
2 Park Square, Milton Park, Abingdon, Oxon, OX14 4RN
and by Routledge
605 Third Avenue, New York, NY 10017

Routledge is an imprint of the Taylor & Francis Group, an informa business

Publisher's Note
The publisher has gone to great lengths to ensure the quality of this reprint but points out that some imperfections in the original copies may be apparent.

Disclaimer
The publisher has made every effort to trace copyright holders and welcomes correspondence from those they have been unable to contact.
A Library of Congress record exists under ISBN: 29003923

For Product Safety Concerns and Information please contact our EU representative:
GPSR@taylorandfrancis.com
Taylor & Francis Verlag GmbH, Kaufingerstraße 24, 80331 München, Germany.

ISBN 13: 978-1-138-55321-7 (hbk)
ISBN 13: 978-1-138-56873-0 (pbk)
ISBN 13: 978-0-203-70482-0 (ebk)

METHODS AND USES
OF
HYPNOSIS AND SELF-HYPNOSIS

METHODS AND USES
OF
HYPNOSIS & SELF-HYPNOSIS

A TREATISE ON THE POWERS OF THE SUBCONSCIOUS MIND

By

BERNARD HOLLANDER

M.D., M.R.C.S., L.R.C.P.

Corresponding Member of the Royal Academy of Medicine of Madrid

LONDON : GEORGE ALLEN & UNWIN LTD
RUSKIN HOUSE, 40 MUSEUM STREET, W.C.1
NEW YORK : THE MACMILLAN COMPANY

First published in 1928

Printed in Great Britain by
Unwin Brothers, Ltd., Woking

PREFACE

The main object of this book is to draw attention to the importance of hypnotism and its phenomena, in order to stimulate inquiry into what is still a mysterious and unexplored subject. This I have already endeavoured to do in an earlier book—*Hypnotism and Suggestion in Daily Life, Education and Medical Practice*—published in 1910, since when I have gained so much additional experience that an entirely new work is necessary.

Having studied hypnotism nearly all my life and practised it for thirty years, the investigations, experiences, and views presented herein should prove of interest and value both to the medical and psychological expert and to the general reader.

Suggestion plays a very important part in our mental development and in our intercourse with our fellows. Life is full of it; we cannot escape its influence. We are constantly receiving suggestions, or suggesting to others, though we are not always conscious of the power we are exercising. Suggestion may be used for self-improvement, and directions will be found herein how to do this most effectively.

In hypnosis, suggestibility is greatly increased. All hypnotic phenomena, however, cannot be explained by suggestion, and certainly do not depend entirely on such a process, but can be produced without its influence. Modern hypnotists rely too much on suggestion, and thereby frustrate their own experiments and fail to produce the extraordinary results achieved by the early mesmerists recorded in this book. For suggestion, whether consciously or unconsciously exercised, is a most potent force, and does not give the innate powers of the subject an opportunity to manifest themselves.

It will be shown in this book that, contrary to common belief, *sleep is quite unnecessary for the induction of hypnosis*. All that is needed is a peculiar state of profound abstraction or absent-mindedness, in which the mind is centred on ideas self-chosen, or presented to it by the operator, to the exclusion of everything else.

In my opinion, based on the results of many experiments, the wonderful phenomena produced in this state depend on the bringing into prominence of what, for convenience, we term the *subconscious mind.* Even in ordinary life, important mental operations are carried on without consciousness—or, at all events, without the full consciousness of the individual; similarly, with the help of hypnotism, the subconscious contents and processes of the mind can be brought into conscious activity and utilized for practical ends. Those of its qualities which make for good can be strengthened; those which make for evil can be weakened. Dormant abilities can be roused to activity, existing faculties exalted, and work accomplished of which the subject was not previously capable.

Indeed, this state resembles that in which men of genius have achieved their highest creations, while completely oblivious of their physical sensations and external surroundings.

It is in this state of passive concentration, when no impression from the external world reaches the brain, that the mind can be directed to the bodily functions and extraordinary physiological results obtained—results leading to *spontaneous and lasting cures*. Such cures are all the more remarkable when it is remembered that hypnotism is not, as a rule, resorted to until all ordinary methods have failed. Such hypnotic treatment is peculiarly successful in *nervous and mental disorders and moral failings*. Even organic disease can be influenced by securing sleep and removing pain.

To make the cures lasting it is absolutely essential to *re-educate the patient*—a task which, in the hypnotic state, is far easier to accomplish than in the waking state. It is when re-education has been neglected and the original cause of the trouble has not been removed that relapses are likely to occur. Re-education is vital. Its success depends not so much upon the operator's knowledge of academic psychology as upon his acquaintance with human nature and his experience of life. In no other branch of therapeutics is it so necessary to individualize, and to adapt one's methods to the idiosyncrasies of the patient, to his individual qualities, constitution, temper, disposition, and the mood he happens to be in at the time. By re-education, rightly applied, the subject can be made healthier, better, and more efficient.

Further, it is shown in this book that the study of hypnotic phenomena brings us nearer to an explanation of such mysterious manifestations as *Thought Transference*, *Clairvoyance*, *Premonitions*, etc. The time is passed when all such phenomena were to be dismissed, or deemed to be produced by self-deception or imposture.

Whatever grounds there may have been for *objections to hypnotic treatment* in the past, they are no longer valid, now that the subject is hardly ever "sent to sleep." Moreover—and I state it most emphatically—by the methods described no subject can be made to do anything to which he is not naturally disposed. Neither is any subject deprived of his will, but the will is directed from the wrong into the right channels. Of course, abuse of hypnosis (as of any other form of treatment) is possible to the unscrupulous; but if the investigation of hypnotism is neglected by qualified medical men to whom a high moral reputation and public esteem is a necessity of existence, we have no guarantee that it may not be practised by immoral and criminal persons.

Hypnotism is no longer a matter for the showman, but for the physician and the psychologist. It is an intensely important and interesting subject, and this book should help all educated people to learn something of its facts. The records given will, I hope, convince the reader that there are forces in human beings the presence of which, with our available knowledge, we can only surmise, and that the strange powers of hypnosis may unlock many doors and lead to the solution of many mysteries.

BERNARD HOLLANDER.

57 Wimpole Street, London, W. 1.
April 1928.

CONTENTS

PAGE

PREFACE 7

CHAPTER

I. UNIVERSAL SUGGESTIBILITY 15

II. THE SUBCONSCIOUS MIND 36

III. EXPLANATION OF HYPNOTISM 50

IV. METHODS OF HYPNOSIS 65

V. THE APPLICATION OF HYPNOTISM TO THE TREATMENT OF BODILY AND MENTAL DISORDERS 82

VI. ACCENTUATION OF THE SENSES FOLLOWING HYPNOSIS 99

VII. EXALTATION OF THE INTELLECTUAL POWERS IN HYPNOSIS 115

VIII. HEIGHTENED SENSIBILITY IN HYPNOSIS. EMANATIONS AND THE HUMAN AURA 132

IX. SUPERNORMAL PHENOMENA : CLAIRVOYANCE, TELEPATHY, APPARITIONS, PREMONITIONS . 147

X. THE OBJECTIONS TO HYPNOTIC TREATMENT . 167

INDEX 181

Hypnosis and Self-Hypnosis

CHAPTER I

UNIVERSAL SUGGESTIBILITY

HITHERTO supernormal powers have been demonstrated only in hypnosis. I shall show that they can be aroused also in the waking state. But since the procedure is very much like hypnosis, some explanation is needed to dispel the misgivings many persons have of submitting themselves, as they erroneously think, to the will of another. It is surprising how many people have a horror of hypnosis. They do not realize that every day they are the subjects of self-hypnosis, and are also influenced by the suggestion of others, without being aware of it.

Suggestibility is a characteristic of human beings; without it social life would be impossible. Everyone is naturally suggestible. We could never think or do anything if we were to wait until each reason for our thoughts or deeds had been proved. Each of us believes in things which he cannot demonstrate, but which he accepts in good faith. It is true that some people boast that they believe only that which is demonstrable to their senses, but the senses often deceive by false perceptions. We are constantly misled, and especially so when we are in a state of expectancy. Thus even renowned men of science, trained to mathematical accuracy, have seen under the microscope that for which they were working, and which, as subsequently proved by others, could not have been there.

Human suggestibility enters into every act of life, colours all our sensations with the most varied tints, leads our judgment astray, and creates those continual illusions against which we have so much difficulty in defending ourselves, even when we exert all the strength of our reason.

We profess to be intelligent human beings; nevertheless, if we were frankly to examine our conscience, we would find that it is difficult always to see clearly, and that daily we are the victims of unreasonable suggestion. As soon as we leave the firm ground of mathematics we experience an incredible difficulty in resisting suggestion. When we formulate an opinion, or when we allow ourselves to be persuaded, it is very rare that logic is the only ground. Our feelings, affection, esteem, the awe and fear which those who are talking to us inspire, surreptitiously prepare the paths of our understanding, and our reason is often taken in a trap. Our sensibility intervenes, our feelings and our secret desires mingle with the cold conception of reason, and, without being conscious of it, we are led into error. We let ourselves be captivated by a superficial eloquence, by the charm of language, and we yield at the first beck of attraction. One person's optimistic reflection can give us strength; the ill-humour of another may take away all our enthusiasm and energy.

Men who pride themselves on their power of resisting external influences are often the most suggestible in every other department of life, except that in which they resolutely determine to be unlike other people. Hence it is not uncommon to find genuine scientific men most credulous in departments of knowledge not their own.

Even the most resolute characters are influenced by suggestion. It only requires that the suggestion should be made artfully. The idea need only be introduced discreetly and gradually in order to succeed. By indirect suggestion the subject has no consciousness that his views are being modified. If a man tells another that Mr. So-and-so, in whom he has complete confidence, is a cheat, the suggestion will be resented; but if he gradually raises a doubt in his friend's mind, the former trust is likely to be shaken. In addition, such new idea introduced almost unnoticed is likely to lie latent for a period, and when it does assert itself it will appear to the subject to have originated with himself.

We are all open to suggestions, some more than others. Some persons are disposed to allow themselves very easily to be influenced by others. On the other hand, we meet people who know how to subject others irresistibly to their influence, and often abuse their gift, if they are unscrupulous.

A message conveying a sudden joy or a great misfortune may produce extraordinary effects beyond all the bounds of reason, and the measure of pleasure we get from life depends more on our suggestibility than on any other factor. Some people can be happy in conditions where others would be miserable, and millionaires have been known to commit suicide because of the loss of a comparatively small portion of their fortune, often merely from fear of loss and not actual loss. Books are bought because of their suggestive titles; fashionable clothes are worn because of the suggestion of wealth and respectability. Certain foods, the habit of open or closed windows, and other idiosyncrasies and hobbies often create pleasure and comfort, or displeasure and discomfort, not because of their actual effects, but by suggestion. A mere suspicion may suffice to set up the greatest agony.

Moreover, suggestion lies at the foundation of all forms of moral and religious teaching. It is, in fact, the basis of education. It has been practised on all of us, sometimes reinforced by the application of more or less violent bodily stimuli, which helped to impress the suggestion more deeply on our minds.

One of the best examples of the effect of suggestion, to the extent of its becoming an obsession, is that of a person who has fallen in love. It is as powerful in its mental and bodily effects as hypnotism. The man or woman who has induced this state of mind exercises a strong fascination over the subject, resulting in complete blindness to the attractions of all other persons and to the physical and mental defects of the object of adoration. Men in love sometimes change the habits of a lifetime, break with their own relations, dismiss their most faithful servants, ruin themselves financially, give up their club and smoking, and may even change their politics and religion. Simultaneously with these mental changes there are certain physical symptoms. In the presence of the object of infatuation a gentle languor pervades the frame; the respiration becomes sighing; the blood rushes to the head, causing a flushing of the countenance. Accompanying this is a great confusion of thought and language, particularly in young persons, and when very acute there may be loss of appetite and insomnia. There is usually a disposition to violent palpitation of the heart and a sensation at times as if the heart had been displaced upwards into the larynx. Persons in love become highly sensitive to each other's feelings. The slightest inattention, or a greeting less warm than usual, will cause serious agitation, worry, and misery, lasting for hours or even days. They become moody and avoid society. If the neglect continues they grow pale and thin, morbid thoughts of self-destruction may arise, and sometimes homicidal impulses at the sight of a rival have been known to occur. On the other hand, a contact of the hands, and even more so of the lips or cheeks, though the action last but a second, may excite feelings of exaltation and happiness of an enduring character. There is no hypnotist who can produce such complex results all at once as are manifest in a person who has "fallen in love."

There are certain classes of persons whose intellectual labours are characterized by suggestibility in a very marked degree. Poets and artists are the most conspicuous examples.

An artist's power depends on how much of his inner nature he can express in his pictures or sculpture to impress the observer. His success depends to some extent on his power to create particular feelings in those who contemplate his work. It will convey different suggestions to different people, and even to the same person at different times the message suggested may vary according to the mood in which he happens to be in. We walk through a city and observe its buildings. What are they? To some they suggest so much stone and lime, iron and timber. To others these structures are embodied ideas, they are permeated with mind, and it is the soul within the material that acts on their subconsciousness.

Of all the works of art none acts so powerfully on our emotions as that of a musical genius. Musical sounds have a mysterious language of their own, which human beings and even some animals intuitively understand, and to which they immediately respond. Apart from the ordinary effects of music we have actual examples in the stirring military band that leads soldiers to fight bravely, when their hearts are perhaps full of fear, and their thoughts with the loved ones at home. We have the powerful organ of the church that moves the man whose belief has perhaps been severely shaken to pray for forgiveness for his sins. When no preacher could bend his spirit sacred music resounding in the lofty, dimly illuminated cathedral will carry his mind to spiritual heights.

When we think of what music contains and what it suggests, we do not wonder that Plato, the great prophet of the ideal, should have put it so high as an element of education and as an inspirer of virtue.

What is true of the painter and music-composer is also true of the writer. Language written or spoken derives its power from what it suggests to us. What can flatter an author more than to hear that his novel has made men and women laugh or weep, or was effective in creating good morals or wicked conduct? After the publication of Goethe's *Sorrows of Werther* there was a perfect epidemic of suicides in Germany.

And what is the object of the dramatist and actor but to suggest certain thoughts and feelings to the audience, and to make them think, laugh, or cry? And although the transferred emotion may be suppressed and is usually not lasting, with a few it is sometimes strong enough to prevent their enjoying supper and sleep that night.

Even in business suggestion plays an important rôle. A good salesman will often dispose of goods that the purchaser had no intention of buying—at any rate, at the price asked. A good buyer often makes a man part with his goods at a figure which the latter may perhaps regret after the transaction is completed. A successful salesman must first gain the customer's attention, then arouse interest and awaken desire, after which the sale may be easily effected.

The art of advertising depends mainly on its power of suggestion. The advertiser may make a simple, bold assertion, and repeat it daily, thus suggesting by its repetition that the statement is true; he may endeavour to catch the sceptic, the man or woman who craves for reason, and may supply it.

In politics, as in daily life, people follow a leader, sometimes against their real interests and convictions. Think of the extraordinary influence of a strong personality like Napoleon, Bismarck, or, say, Gladstone. We have no modern statesman to exercise such a power over his followers, unless it be Mussolini. But if there is no leader in that sense, party leaders have still the same power of acting by suggestion. They give each other bad names in the hope that the voter may be influenced by them. A few cleverly chosen words may suggest a political truth or untruth to a mass of people who do not stop to ascertain their motive or reason, but follow like a flock of sheep.

The power of the Press to produce a desired body of public opinion, merely by the endless repetition of certain carefully chosen phrases, was well illustrated before and during the Great War.

The voter as he reads his newspaper may adopt by suggestion the words which are made habitual by repetition every morning, conveying not only political opinions, but whole trains of political arguments.

The tactics of election politics also depend on the principle of suggestion. The candidate is advised to "show himself" continually, to distribute his portrait periodically, to give away prizes, to "say a few words" at the end of other people's speeches—all under circumstances which offer little or no opportunity for the formation of a reasoned opinion of his merits, but many opportunities for the rise of a purely instinctive affection amongst those present by mere suggestion. (Graham Wallas, *Human Nature in Politics.*)

Just as in the Middle Ages there arose epidemics of hysteria, so it sometimes happens that a whole country has lost its political judgment by some powerful suggestion that blows like a wind of folly over the land. The French Revolution is an example.

History, and more particularly the history of civilization, affords striking instances of the mighty effects of suggestion. Whether we are dealing with social, religious, or political events, or with artistic tendencies and currents of scientific thought, the suggestibility of crowds throws light on many phenomena.

It is feeling, not reason, that sways large gatherings of people. Mobs will commit acts that no member of them would think of perpetrating individually. These whirlpools of emotional excitement are created by the constantly repeated suggestions of those participating in them.

That is how "enthusiasm" is infectious; that is why a theatrical performance is enjoyed more when the house is filled "to capacity" than when half empty.

Suggestion is the cause of the movements and actions of crowds. A word or cry may seize a whole mass of people in its suggestive grasp, so that it is carried away to acts of destruction like a wild and frantic herd. A voice in a dense crowd will not attract attention; but let this crowd stand still and be quiet, that same voice may influence the people. It is an illustration of the same law, which will be explained later, when we deal with the Methods of Hypnotism and with Thought-transference.

That a suggestion may be successful, the receiver must be in a passive, relaxed state. If the receiver is active a suggestion gets no hold upon him, his brain being too much occupied with its own ideas. So also the excited crowd will sweep away the individual, but a passive crowd may be moved by a single voice. One voice speaks and a thousand men and women, gathered promiscuously and knowing nothing of each other, cease to be individuals. They are blended for the time being into a common consciousness, which laughs and cries, exults or despairs as one.

Just as a hypnotized person does not stop to inquire whether the suggestion has a basis of fact, but acts upon it at once, so a passive crowd can be moved suddenly. Let a person in a theatre call out "Fire!" and the audience will not stop to see whether the place is actually burning, but, the feeling of self-preservation being at once aroused, will rush for the doors.

Our character acts on us as a constant suggestion. Every man, of necessity, sees other men and Nature itself through the prism of his own individuality. Thus the pessimist is convinced deeply that evil is everywhere, when it is, in fact, within himself. Hence the value of having an ideal, some aspiration, whereby to oppose the suggestiveness of inherent characteristics and attractive temptations, and to shape our conduct with the voluntarily chosen goal.

It is a peculiarity of the subconscious mind that it is highly amenable to suggestion. It *receives* suggestions not only from external sources, but from the conscious mind itself, and it *gives* suggestions not only from our past experiences, but from the experiences transmitted from our forefathers. Looked at in this light, heredity may be regarded as a mass of potent suggestions transmitted from our ancestors. *We do not inherit qualities ready-made, such as virtues and vices; we only get from our parents more or less well-constituted brains, capable of reacting more or less promptly and accurately to the various stimuli which cause their activity.* Suppose, for instance, an infant to be born with a predominant tendency to the feeling of fear; that feeling, as reason develops, will become intellectualized; and, if no counteracting tendency is present, it will form the ruling idea for his guidance, it will act as a potent suggestion, and his characteristic will be *circumspection.*

And so all our deep-seated feelings and instincts can become intellectual qualities, which we think we make for ourselves, whereas in reality they are hereditary suggestions to determine our conduct.

Children are almost purely subjective; and no one needs to be told how completely a suggestion, true or false, will take control of their minds. Their good manners are easily destroyed by bad company, and their minds can be corrupted by what they see, hear, and read.

Looked at in this manner it will be seen that we are a mass of suggestions—suggestions from within and suggestions from without. One can overcome the other, but it may be laid down at once that external suggestions act on us more readily when they are in harmony with our internal ones—that is, when they are in harmony with those auto-suggestions which conform with our natural character. When the subconscious mind is confronted by two opposing suggestions the hereditary auto-suggestion and a suggestion from another person, the stronger necessarily prevails. Thus a man with settled moral principles will successfully resist the suggestions of crime and immorality; for his moral principles constitute auto-suggestions, the strength of which is proportionate to that of his moral character.

Suggestion in the widest sense can be direct or indirect, but direct persuasion is not usually regarded as suggestion. As Professor Bechterev has cleverly said: "Suggestion enters into the understanding by the back stairs, while logical persuasion knocks at the front door." Suggestion, in this more restricted sense, is a process of communication of an idea to the subconscious mind in an unobtrusive manner, carrying conviction, when consciously there is no inclination to accept it, and logically there are no adequate grounds for its acceptance.

The expression "suggestion" betokens nothing more than an idea selected by ourselves and prominently held before the mind, or conveyed from outside sources and accepted by us because more or less in harmony with our own ideas and dispositions and prevailing moods, and forming the initial point of further process of thought, or leading to action in accordance with the object of the idea.

All persons are more or less amenable to suggestion, not merely in hypnosis, but in the ordinary waking condition. Examples have been given of this universal susceptibility. Other illustrations are: gaping involuntarily, even against one's strenuous attempts to avoid it, on seeing another yawn; beating time unconsciously on hearing the measured throb of martial music; becoming wildly excited for no other reason than that one's companions are panic-stricken; and, contrariwise, having one's fears allayed by the tranquil demeanour of associates in a terrible emergency. With many people the mere statement that they are blushing is enough to produce a flow of blood to the face; the repeated assurance that they are warm or cold will tend to make them feel warmer or colder; the mention or the sight of certain little insects seldom fails to make the skin itch uncomfortably.

By far the greater number of pleasures and of pains comes from suggestion, and not from the direct action of the stimuli upon the senses. Suggestibility is increased in illness, in fatigue, and periods of mental tension—in all states, in short, that tend to obscure or divert the reasoning function. These are conditions of emotional susceptibility; the emotions become more acute, and the emotions dazzle, they do not enlighten, the understanding. One sees more clearly in fair weather than in storm. In periods of depression we are especially open to unhappy suggestions, and in periods of success to all that is hopeful and promising.

The power suggestion has over us depends largely on the attention we pay to it. Many a patient would recover more quickly if he did not increase his painful sensations by dwelling on them and constantly send anxious thought currents to the diseased organ. Half the ills of mankind may be described as mental ills, and even the organic ills are considerably aggravated by our apprehensions and fears regarding them. We cannot always help our thoughts, but we need not dwell on them. It is our own thought direction which is instrumental in causing misery, disease, and trouble of all sorts.

We are constantly suggesting to ourselves. Such suggestion originating within the individual we call *auto-suggestion*. It may be either a suggestion from the conscious self to the subconscious self—a self-imposed narrowing of the field of consciousness to one idea by holding a given thought in the mental focus to the exclusion of all other thoughts, so that antagonistic psychic combinations do not come into play, as, for instance, when concentrating before going to sleep on the one thought to rise the next morning punctually at seven o'clock; or it may be a suggestion arising from the subconsciousness, owing to hereditary ancestral tendencies or acquired experiences, and dictating to the consciousness, such as the fear suggested to many people when they sleep in a remotely situated, empty house.

All self-suggestions we deliberately make to ourselves, if to be successful, should be made when in an absolutely tranquil state. If the mind is centred so that no external impression rouses it, and there is no activity and no conflict of other faculties, the suggested idea will reach the subconscious and work itself out. The last thing before going to sleep is a good time for auto-suggestion, for there is a certain emptiness of mind and suspension of the mental faculties. When a person seeks repose in sleep he has recourse to darkness and silence, shuts his eyes to cut off all visual impressions, stretches himself out comfortably in order to relax his muscles completely, covers himself over to protect himself from cold or other sensations, and tries to dismiss from his mind all disturbing thoughts; in short, he isolates himself where nothing can distract his senses or excite his mind. In so doing he releases all that attention which had been employed previously in producing different sensations, movements, and ideas, and is in a fit condition to focus on the desired object, which then makes the required impression on his brain.

The first suggestion should be an easy one, such as to wake at a definite time. Most people can do that readily. Having succeeded in this, we can then add other suggestions. For example, the depressed man may wish to wake up cheerful, singing, or whistling, not knowing the reason why; the worrying man may pray to wake free from apprehension, or that he will have forgotten certain harassing events of the past; and any task that ought to be attended to, but has been neglected, can be willed to be carried out at a definite time, even with the right inspiration if we have hitherto lacked the proper decision.

The suggestions should be as brief as possible and be dismissed as soon as made. Suggestions should not be repeated in parrot fashion, as was done in Coué's method, for repetition fatigues the particular brain centres and lessens the efficiency of the suggestion. Coué's repetition of the formula, "Day by day, in every way, I am getting better and better," was applicable chiefly to the large number of self-hypnotized people who persuaded themselves that they never would be any better. Having given the order to the subconscious, we should not think any more about it, but should switch off on to some pleasant subject of contemplation. The order is given and dismissed from consciousness until it is realized. It is precisely this unawareness of the process which distinguishes suggestion from an ordinary act of volition, from one wherein the subject realizes his idea through conscious effort and while uninterruptedly supervising the work of performance. It is just like the process of remembering a name when all voluntary effort has failed. If one switches off to another subject, the name may flash into consciousness some time later, though no further attempt has been made to recall it. It is the same as when we decide to sleep over a difficulty, when the right decision may be arrived at in the morning.

Suggestion is greatly helped by picturing the expected condition—the condition one wishes to bring about, so that the subconscious may realize physically the visualized thought-picture. Thus, in a case of stage-fright, we may imagine ourselves beforehand facing the audience and addressing it in the right bodily attitude, full of courage and determination. When we later actually face the people we are familiar with the aspect and less likely to experience fear.

Mental discipline is very helpful, for our dominating thoughts determine our dominating actions. Whatever we intend to do, we should be prepared in thought for it. Whatever we would not do, we must look to it that we do not entertain the type of thought that will give birth to the act. If we do not will our own thoughts, the brain will manufacture thoughts which are not of our choosing. It should be a rule to have a time for everything and to keep to it as much as is humanly possible. Even the suggestions should be associated with definite times, for instance, "I shall remember at four o'clock to do so and so." Wishes associated with definite times are much more likely to be realized than when expressed vaguely.

Mental discipline includes emotional discipline. We should choose a time for auto-suggestion when we are free from disturbing emotions. Many a man goes in for memory training to become mentally efficient, when it would be much more to the purpose if he learned emotional control in order to acquire the power of concentration. Uncertainty, anxiety, worry, and fear hinder intellectual work; but we can do an enormous amount of it when, instead of these feelings, the mind is filled with calmness, assurance, courage, and confidence. Many a student who knows his work well, when facing the examiner is so anxious about the result or so full of fear that he cannot remember the simplest thing, yet on leaving the examination room he remembers all again and could answer every question perfectly. Another student does not care anything about the examiner or the result of the examination, and may not have learnt half as much, yet, being free from emotion, he is able to command the little knowledge he does possess and make the most of it, and he passes successfully.

Auto-suggestion is greatly facilitated by the right emotional condition. Many persons who feel the need of such help find it difficult to produce that mood which would make suggestion effective. Let such persons read a stimulating book, or go to a play which is elevating, or let them in any other way evoke those favourable emotions which will give energy to their ideas. Thus reinforced they will find that their suggestions will have greater vigour and certainty of realization.

If a thought can in an instant of time dilate or contract a blood-vessel; if it can increase or decrease the secretion of a gland; if it can hasten or retard the action of the heart; if it can turn the hair grey in a single night; if it can force tears from the eyes; if it can in an instant produce great bodily weakness; if it can produce insomnia—we need not be surprised that the suggestion of thought can produce similar effects and influence the bodily functions for good. What mind can cause mind can cure. After all, it is Nature that heals, the doctor only facilitates the process. For instance, the surgeon does not mend a broken leg; he only puts it into the posture and the condition which enables Nature to mend it. Surgical direction is necessary, but the patient's thoughts can accelerate as well as retard the process. Of course, faith goes a long way. Often it is not the medicine which cures, but faith in the physician who prescribed it. That is why a doctor may be able to cure one person of a disorder or disease and be powerless with another suffering from the very same trouble.

Some men have the power of exciting belief in others, whether we call it personal magnetism or by any other name. It is a gift. Some people inspire hope, induce faith, and bestow comfort. A gentle hand and a gentle voice have often done wonders, even in the case of the unskilled. The alleged cures performed through the agency of sacred relics, at holy shrines, at Lourdes, and other wonder-working centres, are wrought almost wholly among a certain type of people, who are ready to accept the particular belief with all the energy of their being.

If ignorant and superstitious people can be cured quickly because they are credulous, if cures of all kinds and among all classes depend on the faith or confidence put into the remedial means, is there not some deeper law which governs all cases, by the discovery of which the intelligent can be cured as quickly as the superstitious?

Every healer, whether a qualified physician or a layman, consciously or unconsciously uses suggestion in some form; but this does not always suffice. Similarly, many people willing to use auto-suggestion are unsuccessful. Often the latter have got into the habit of contrary self-hypnotization and cannot suggest to themselves against the prevalent groove of thoughts. All such people require the assistance of one skilled in the practice of suggestion and psychotherapy, and some special form of procedure to impress them.

Of course, suggestion and suggestibility are not

real causes. They are simply the means to designate facts themselves, of which we must seek the causes. For this purpose we must understand, first of all, the nature of consciousness and subconsciousness.

CHAPTER II

THE SUBCONSCIOUS MIND

Consciousness is that mental state in which we are aware of our existence and sensations, and the condition at the moment of our thoughts, feelings, and actions. Consciousness means *awareness*; we are not aware of things of which we are not conscious. When there is only one response possible to a sensation, we get automatic (reflex) action, and consciousness, if aroused at all, is slight. The greater the complexity of the nervous system, the more numerous the possible responses to a sensation, the greater will be the hesitation and choice, and the more intense the consciousness.

Consciousness develops gradually, and *self-consciousness*, i.e. the process of directing the attention inwards to the mental self, is its highest degree. Thus the new-born babe, whose existence alternates between drinking and sleeping, is unconscious of anything but a few sensations. Its consciousness is very vague and develops gradually, until it reaches self-consciousness, the recognition of itself as distinct from the outer world, and the appreciation of the nature and quality of its acts. Self-consciousness has the character of continuity, being connected with the past through the memory, and is the feeling which we have that the mental processes belong to our personality.

Consciousness runs in personal streams, so long as the brain is stable. As the brain grows, decays, or is influenced by various agents, so will consciousness vary; but the main character, the main self, always remains behind these variations, even in cases of dual personality. Such dissociation of consciousness may occur in hysteria, epilepsy, and may be produced artificially in hypnotism, but all these conditions are only superficial and temporary, the real personality is not destroyed so long as the brain does not suffer permanent injury.

Our inherited dispositions—our primary innate capacities, rudimentary emotions, and instinctive tendencies—are all *unconscious*. Only after their manifestation, by reflection on our impulses and conduct, do we become aware of them, and can determine to control them in future. For example, I cannot say, "I am going to 'fear' now." The youth attracted by the maiden does not know why he follows her; he is unconscious of the racial instinct which urges him.

In addition to our unconscious motive powers—the instincts and emotions which we share with the lower animals and which depend on peculiarities of brain structure—we all have a store of experiences, accumulated from birth and registered in our brain cells, so that they are never lost, though we may experience difficulties in recalling them. This available material constitutes our stock of knowledge and our history. It is also unconscious; but being possible of recall, we say, for distinction sake, it is *subconscious*.

We can attend only to one thing at a time; all the rest is removed from consciousness, though it can be used whenever required.

Consciousness is only a phase of our psychical life; but not the psychical life itself. So far as there is consciousness there is certainly mental activity; but it is not true that in the same measure as there is mental activity there is consciousness. *There is a thousand times more below the surface of consciousness than there is above.* We flatter ourselves that it is we who are thinking; whereas the thinking is within us and goes on all the time. We do the thinking only when absolutely conscious.

Every impression we receive, every thought we think, every action we do, causes some change in the brain structure, and this change is permanent. It forms an imperishable record of all that we have experienced, thought, or done in the past, and exercises an influence over us, building up our present knowledge, and guiding our everyday actions. Many minds are moody, morose, melancholy, excitable, immoral, unbalanced, solely because of the overpowering influence of some picture of past experience, which remains subconsciously in operation after conscious thought on the occurrence has ceased and the person has apparently forgotten the incident. What we call "common sense" is nothing but a reservoir of experiences out of which our judgments flow, while the experiences themselves are hidden away in the subconscious depths of our intellectual nature.

The mystery of subconscious mental action is exemplified in every act of mental association, when one idea brings up another, of which we are wholly unconscious.

All our latent memories, possible ideas, and materials of imagination are stored in our subconscious mind. Not a millionth part of the mental possessions of an educated man exists in his consciousness at any one time. We may forget objects and events—that is to say, we may dismiss them from our consciousness—but they are stored up in our subconsciousness (impressed upon our brain cells) to the end of our days, and supply the mind with its resources. We may be able to call them into consciousness by some association when we wish to do so, or they may flash into consciousness for some reason without any effort of ours, but at other times the mind is unconscious of their existence.

There are thoughts which never emerge into consciousness, which yet make their influence felt among the perceptible mental currents. Our social predilections, religious and other beliefs and prejudices instilled in childhood, colour our whole being. Indeed, the more we examine the mechanism of thought the more we shall see that the subconscious contents of the mind enters largely into all its processes. *Hypnosis is one of the means of getting at the subconscious contents and teaching the subject how to use this store voluntarily to great effect, to accomplish what the conscious mind failed to achieve.*

Some psychologists argue that there is no subconsciousness; but we have no other expression for those experiences, thoughts, and emotions which are not in consciousness at any given moment, and use the term—subconscious—only as a working hypothesis, not as an entity. Whether we admit an absolute unconsciousness or a relative unconsciousness or subconsciousness, a subliminal consciousness or a secondary consciousness, or a fringe of consciousness, does not matter much at the present stage, so long as we are agreed that conscious experiences are relegated to another region, or, at least, do not remain in consciousness, but are capable of being *revived* in consciousness. We know that the man of genius derives his brilliant thoughts from that mysterious source; the inventor and discoverer, his guidance; the poet, his inspiration; the religious man, his beliefs.

The essential principle of thinking is that the right ideas occur at the right time. On sitting down to write an essay or letter we often do not know what we are going to say; but from the moment of taking the pen in hand our subconscious store of ideas supplies us with the material. We have a name for such moments—we call them inspired; and thus erroneously go outside ourselves for an explanation, instead of finding it in our subconscious mind. It is in the subconscious mind that the germs of such ideas were sown, perchance, far back in our childhood, developed by our surroundings, added to by conditions beyond our control, and not chosen by those who were preparing the material for our mental development.

Most of our thinking is done subconsciously. As a rule we are conscious only of the *result* of a mental exercise; the actual origin and working remain obscure. For instance, we may try to solve a problem and fail, but when we have given up the task an idea may suddenly dawn upon us that leads to its solution, showing that subconscious processes continued the work. Even in the conscious act of perception through our senses there is a subconscious process of reproduction and influence; hence the liability of all of us at one time or another to be the subjects of hallucination. Indeed, even in the cleverest of us, in the ordinary mental operations of our daily life, there is not so much consciousness as is commonly assumed. Unconsciously and subconsciously we constantly believe in things which do not exist, or exist only in part. That we distrust consciousness, at all events in important matters, is shown by the wish to "sleep over" a matter, not only that our conscious processes may be clearer, but that we may have the help of that unformulated knowledge which, at most, can be said to be only in the background of consciousness. In important matters we often feel confident that a certain course is the right one—as we know a road or face without being able to describe it—but cannot formulate the ground for decision in words.

There are many events which are so completely forgotten that no efforts of the will can revive them, and the statement of them calls up no reminiscences, which may nevertheless be reproduced with intense vividness under certain physical conditions. Thus persons in the delirium of fever have been known to speak in a language which they had learned in their childhood, but which for many years had passed from their memory; or to repeat with apparent accuracy discourses to which they had listened a long time previously, but of which before the fever they had no recollection. They have even been known to repeat accurately long passages from books in foreign languages of which they never had any understanding and no recollection in normal health, but which they had casually heard recited many years before.

A case is related by S. T. Coleridge of a young woman of five-and-twenty who could neither read nor write, and who was seized with "brain fever" during which she continued incessantly talking Latin, Greek, and Hebrew in very pompous tones, and with a most distinct enunciation. Notes of her ravings were taken down from her own mouth, and later it was found that she had been for some years servant to a Protestant pastor, who was in the habit of walking up and down a passage of his house adjoining the kitchen reading aloud to himself portions of his favourite authors. In the books that had belonged to him were found many passages identical with those taken down from the girl's unconscious utterances.

In the course of my practice of hypnotism I have several times revived the memory of a long-forgotten event in a hypnotized subject, and sometimes of a piece of poetry of which the subject had no recollection in the normal state and which I had not heard or read before, thus excluding the possibility of transference of thought. The most remarkable cases, however, are those of persons resuscitated from drowning and who have reported that they had a sudden revelation of all the events of their past life presented to them with the utmost minuteness and distinctness just before consciousness left them.

An act of attention, that is an act of concentration—by which we mean the fixing of the mind intently upon one particular object to the exclusion for the time of all other objects that solicit its notice—is necessary to every exertion of consciousness. Without some degree of attention no impression of any duration can be made on the mind or laid up in the memory. The remembrance of anything depends upon the clearness and vividness of the impression originally made by it upon the mind, and this in turn on the degree of attention with which it was regarded. Consciousness has at first an important place in the training of our faculties and the building up of our knowledge. The more consciousness is concentrated upon any new subject, the more readily is it mastered; and the greater the concentration upon any idea brought before the mind, the better its impression upon the memory. But as we acquire facility and skill in the operation, and as the memory acquires strength, we become less conscious.

Acts which are at first executed slowly, and with full consciousness and attention, become gradually less and less perceptible as they gain in ease and rapidity by repetition, till they fall below the minimum necessary for consciousness, and become unconscious, or rather subconscious. It is because impressions we have frequently received, thoughts we have often entertained, actions we have many times performed, pass through the mind so rapidly that we cease to be conscious of them. In our attempts to walk, to write, to play on an instrument, or to carry on any other operation, we are intensely conscious of every movement that we make. By degrees, as we acquire more ease and dexterity in their performance, we become less and less conscious of them, till we may come to perform them quite unconsciously. The great object of mental training, therefore, should be to transfer as much as possible of our actions from the conscious to the subconscious region of the mind.

Did our actions not become more and more easy of execution, and gain in rapidity by repetition, were we still as conscious of them as at first, comparatively little could be accomplished in the course of a lifetime. If, in order to walk, we had for ever carefully to consider each step we took, or, in order to write, had always to attend to the formation of each letter —were all our other operations performed as painfully and as consciously as at first—life could scarcely fail to be a burden.

If everything that exists in the mind existed there consciously, or if every time that an idea occurred to the mind all the other ideas that had at any time

been associated with it came along with it, and a selection had to be consciously made of the right one, inconvenience and loss of time would unfailingly result. In some persons, from habit or lack of proper training, an idea presented to the mind immediately recalls a number of other ideas, having more or less, sometimes very little, connection with it—thus distracting the mind with a multitude of thoughts, making the selection of the best a conscious act, producing hesitation and indecision and causing loss of time. The selection of the right thoughts should be an act of the subconscious mind, and take place, as we say, unconsciously.

The more we concentrate our attention on a particular subject, the less we notice our concurrent impressions. For example, in listening to a conversation, we receive impressions, not only of the words uttered, but also of the sounds in the air, and of its temperature, of odours, the forms, colours, lights and shades—all associating themselves with the thoughts conveyed—but we exclude all these impressions from our consciousness, although they may be noticed by our subconsciousness.

The more we concentrate on a subject, the less we notice also our internal sensations. Hence, in times of real danger, the body may feel no pain, no matter how severe the injury. The universal testimony of soldiers who have been in battle is to the effect that the time when fear is experienced is just before the action commences. When the first gun is fired all fear vanishes, and the soldier often performs feats of the most desperate valour, and evinces the most reckless courage. If wounded, he feels nothing until the battle is over and all excitement is gone.

Ordinarily, when we concentrate our attention, we nevertheless take note of the room we are in, its furniture, the decoration of the walls, and perhaps also of our internal sensations. Concentration is, therefore, rarely complete. We shall show how absolute concentration can be produced with freedom from all other impressions, and that in this absorbed state the power of whatever sense is employed is greatly increased and perceptions are possible, which escape us in the ordinary state of concentration. Moreover, whatever innate ability is employed will produce results to the utmost capacity of the particular brain structure, which is its instrument.

In dealing with mind and consciousness we must remember that they are in some mysterious manner related to the outer surface, the grey matter of the brain, which consists of millions of cells, so-called neurons, the functions of which physiologists all over the world are trying to determine. The most important point on which they are all agreed is that the brain is the structure through which all mental operations take place. We think and feel, rejoice and weep, love and hate, hope and fear, trust and suspect, plan and execute, all through the agency of the brain-cortex. Its cells record all the events, of whatever nature, which transpire within the sphere of existence of the individual, not merely as concerns the intellectual knowledge acquired, but likewise the emotions felt and the passions indulged in, whether he recollects them or not.

But the brain, besides being an organ of mind, is also the regulator of all the functions of the body, the controller of every organ. For this purpose it has two sets of nerves: firstly, the *cerebro-spinal* nerves, which in the normal state are more or less under our voluntary control, enabling us to move our muscles and limbs; and secondly, the so-called *sympathetic* nerves, which are not under our conscious volition. The sympathetic nerves go to our internal organs as well as our arteries, controlling the local blood supply and consequently nutrition, and go also to the spinal nerves, thus exerting a brain control over intentional movements. In the manner roughly outlined every organ and every function is represented in the brain, and in such a manner that all may be brought into the right relationship and harmony with each other and constitute a vital unity. Thus mind, motion, sensibility, nutrition, drainage, and repair have their governing centres in the brain.

When the response to an external stimulus is effected through the voluntary or cerebro-spinal system, there results a motion, a movement. When the response is effected through the involuntary or sympathetic nervous system, there results a feeling or emotion. The cerebro-spinal system of nerves is thus commonly associated with voluntary, purposive acts, with consciousness, thought, will, and the agreeable and expanding emotions, such as joy; while the sympathetic nervous system is associated with unconscious acts which, when we become aware of them, we recognize as contracting and painful emotions, such as fear or anger. Important discoveries have been made within recent years proving that the sympathetic nervous system stimulates the secretion of certain glands, the ductless glands; and that this secretion in turn increases the sympathetic response and affects our emotions. Thoughts come and go; emotions last some time. When, for example, the emotion of fear is aroused, it may continue even when danger is passed.

Every form of psychotherapy depends on the fact that bodily functions can be affected by a mental act. Not only can certain abnormal mental states derange the functions of the body, but when a healthy state of mind is induced the functional derangements tend to disappear. On the other hand, our mental dispositions can be influenced by the bodily functions. That is one of the reasons why no person is constantly the same self. Not only is he a different self at different periods of his life and in altered circumstances, but also on separate days, according to his varying bodily states; sanguine and optimistic, gloomy and pessimistic, frank and genial, reserved and suspicious, apathetic or energetic. Although his intellectual powers remain the same, his judgment of the objective world and his relations to it are changed, because of the change in his moods and the bodily states which they imply.

Often it happens that a person cannot remember the event which caused the emotional disturbance and deranged the bodily and—may be—the mental functions. If he does remember he may be unable to dismiss the memory of it. By the procedure which we call hypnosis lost memories which have been relegated to the subconscious can be restored, experiences which were almost or entirely subconscious can be recalled, and a normal mental state substituted for the disturbing one.

CHAPTER III

EXPLANATION OF HYPNOTISM

CONSIDERING that we possess little or no knowledge of what mind itself is, it can cause no wonder that all the explanations offered hitherto for the phenomena of hypnotism are still unsatisfactory. Because in the deeper states of hypnosis we notice a condition similar to sleep, hypnotists have identified hypnosis with a peculiar form of sleep. But, as will be shown in succeeding chapters, most of the phenomena can be produced in the waking state.

The word "hypnosis" conveys the idea of sleep, but for the present we have no other term to take its place. This is a pity, for even the deepest hypnosis is not really sleep. The subject becomes more or less unconscious that he has a body, and, if his attention is drawn to it, it will feel heavy and immobile, so long as no suggestion is made to the contrary; but the mind is always awake, only concentrated almost exclusively on the operator, his words and actions. If we ask the subject whether he is asleep he will invariably deny it. Indeed, some subjects interrupt the proceeding with the exclamation: "Doctor, I am still wide awake!" unless we have explained to them beforehand that hypnosis and sleep are not identical.

We may induce hypnosis by suggesting that sleep will come; but the fact that belief in sleep and the expectation of it bring with them the hypnotic state is not a proof that the state itself is sleep. The hypnotic state may be brought about by fascination, as by staring at a glaring light, or by passes made with the operator's hands over the subject's face or body; in either case without the person knowing that the intention is to send him to sleep or produce hypnosis.

The hypnotic state in some ways resembles sleep, but that does not justify us in regarding it as such. It can be brought about by the same influences and conditions that produce sleep, such as the withdrawal of all strong stimuli, a restful position, the monotonous, gentle stimulation of one or more of the special sense organs, expectation, banishment of certain thoughts, or the concentration of attention on some unexciting object or sense impression. In hypnosis, as in sleep, the subject is inert and passive. On the other hand, normal sleep is often induced in the same manner as hypnotic sleep. Children, when their sleep does not come naturally, are often talked or sung to, or rocked to sleep. Grown-up people, too, produce the hypnotic state in themselves by concentrating their minds upon the thought and expectation of sleep, or at least by excluding all disturbing and exciting thoughts.

As far as we know, in natural sleep consciousness is lost completely, in hypnotic sleep it is not; for though the subject may not remember on waking what has occurred, he recollects everything when he is again hypnotized, so that the recollection from one hypnotic sleep to another is continuous.

In all probability hypnosis is purely a psychical state, whereas natural sleep is dependent on changes in the circulation and chemistry of the brain, or at least on physiological processes. Under hypnotic suggestion people fall asleep without fatigue to help them, and may be made to sleep so deeply that even surgical operations on them do not waken them, while ordinary sleep needs to be helped on by fatigue and other physiological changes, and is often hindered by pain and pathological inhibitions.

During sleep, the pulse, respiration, and other bodily functions are modified, but they are not in hypnosis, save in exceptional circumstances. In hypnosis the subject remains *en rapport* with the operator or some other person who may make suggestions; whereas in ordinary sleep, as soon as consciousness is lost, the subject loses connections with the outside world. Ordinary sleep is too deep to make the influence of suggestion possible, though cases are on record in which dreams have been suggested to persons in light sleep, so that their natural sleep was converted into hypnotic sleep. When falling into ordinary sleep the mind passes from one idea to another indifferently, and the subject is unable to fix his attention on any regular train of thought, or to perform any act requiring much voluntary effort. On the other hand, the concentration of attention, which is the result of means employed for inducing hypnosis, is continued into the state itself, and verbal suggestions or sensory impressions excite definite trains of thought or physical movements instead of dreams.

In both normal and hypnotic sleep only part of the brain may be at rest, while the remainder, if not actually awake, may be easily aroused. Thus a mother may sleep peacefully in spite of her husband's worst snores, yet wake at the slightest whisper from her infant. The same partial sleep can be produced in hypnosis. For example, Forel, when director of the Asylum for the Insane at Zürich, was able to induce deep sleep in certain attendants, and yet make them notice any movement on the part of patients dangerous to themselves or others. The slightest activity would immediately wake them.

The hypnotic state has been compared with the dream state; but in dreams the mind is relaxed, the thoughts are confused, and events and sensations pass through the mind in kaleidoscopic succession. In hypnosis, on the other hand, the concentration of attention, which is the result of the means employed for inducing hypnosis, is continued into the state itself, and verbal suggestions or sensory impressions excite definite trains of thought or physical movements instead of dreams. Another difference is that the intellectual activity of the dream consciousness is marked by an absence of logical consistency and moral censorship; whereas in hypnosis the capacity for logical thought is preserved, and moral consciousness is not only retained but heightened.

On the other hand, there are certain analogies between dream consciousness and the hypnotic state. It is a characteristic of dreams that the most improbable things are accepted by us without question. We have become so credulous that all the images which present themselves to our minds, however absurd they may be, are received as real without difficulty. In normal waking life a man can convince himself of the inaccuracy of a statement by means of his senses; and, apart from this, an idea in itself has the same tendency that it has in dreams and in deep hypnosis to develop into a hallucination which dims the judgment. In dreams we believe that what we see or feel are real objects; our sense impressions do not procure normal perceptions but illusions, and the power of judging the experiences of which we are conscious is essentially altered. These peculiarities are also common to consciousness in hypnosis.

In deep hypnosis the resisting consciousness is absent. True, a subject may resist the suggestion of an operator, and frequently does so; but it is a subconscious resistance through the habits which have been formed by him, which the suggestion has, so to say, offended. The existing consciousness being absent, the suggestion is at once transformed into action. The hypnotized person in that state may, therefore, be compared to a somnambulist.

When a subject in hypnosis has accepted a suggestion, he will still use whatever there is within range of his own knowledge or experience, whatever he has seen, heard, or read, which confirms or illustrates that idea; but he is apparently totally oblivious of all facts or ideas which do not confirm, and are not in accord with, the one central idea. A hypnotized person in that state never uses inductive reasoning; his reasoning is always deductive.

There are other analogies between dream consciousness and the phenomena of hypnotism. For instance, it is well known that the recollection of what occurred during hypnotic sleep is in exact inverse proportion to the depth of the sleep. If the sleep is light, the remembrance of the subject is perfect. If the sleep is profound, he remembers nothing, no matter what the character of the scenes he may have passed through. The same is true of dreams. We remember only those dreams which occur during the period when we are just going to sleep or are just awakening. Profound sleep is dreamless, so far as the recollection of the sleeper informs him. Further, as in dreams we often assume a different personality, so in deep hypnosis a subject can be made to change his identity—that is to say, he can be made to forget who he is, and whatever name or character is suggested to a subject is at once assumed and carried out with all the deductive logical attitude characteristic of subjective reasoning. It is also well known that the subject can be made to assume any number of characters by the same process.

The prevalent theory is that the state of hypnosis

is due to suggestion, and the power of suggestion is explained by the suggestibility of the subject. This explanation leads us nowhere. It is comparable with the reason given why opium produces sleep, because opium has a sleep-producing virtue.

Under suggestion have been grouped the invocation of the gods by the Egyptian priests; the sympathetic powder of Paracelsus; the King's touch for the cure of special diseases; the wonderful "cures" at Lourdes; the miraculous power supposed to reside in the relics of the saints; the equally miraculous cures of such men as Greatrakes, Gassner, and of the Abbot Prince of Hohenlohe, and all the modern systems of mind and faith cure.

The word "suggestion" has been too generally adopted as if it explained all mysteries. When the subject obeys it is by reason of the operator's suggestion; when he proves refractory, it is in consequence of an auto-suggestion which he has made to himself. Even the chemical and physical action of medicinal remedies is sometimes denied, and their results traced to suggestion. That which explains everything explains nothing. What really needs explanation is that in a certain condition of the subject suggestions operate as they do at no other time, and that through them functions are affected which ordinarily elude the action of the waking will.

There is one vastly important fact with regard to all psychic healing, and that is the marvellous cures which are constantly effected through its agencies.

To the casual observer it would appear self-evident that underlying all there must be some one principle —the operation of mind on the body—which, once understood, would show them to be identical as to cause and mode of operation. It will be seen from the evidence which will be given that, just as spontaneous healing sometimes takes place when light hypnosis is induced purely through emotional agencies, so "miraculous healing" is sometimes apparently accomplished by the calming of disturbing emotions which hinder the normal working of the nervous system, and the stimulation of elevating emotions which increase the trophic and healing power of the nervous system.

Hypnotism is not all subjective, all due to suggestion, and therefore a mere extension of the ordinary influence which one mind has over another. Suggestion alone does not explain the influencing of subjects without their knowledge; nor is it compatible with the definite physiological effects upon the muscles, the circulation, and the secretions which have been proved to take place; nor does it explain how children too young to understand what is expected of them, and animals of various kinds, can be hypnotized.

In hypnosis suggestibility is greatly increased. A similar suggestible state is also met with in persons as the result of certain conditions, such as great bodily fatigue. People are always more suggestible at the beginning of sleep, and it is also known that in the first stages of chloroform narcosis the patient can be influenced by suggestion. But hypnosis is not necessarily conditioned by suggestion. I have frequently left boys alone in a room gazing at a glass crystal, making no other remarks but that I would come back in ten or twenty minutes—would they meanwhile keep their eyes fixed on the crystal—and when I returned I found them in the cataleptic state. It is possible, of course, that these boys may have had the knowledge that crystal-gazing may induce sleep; but so far as I could ascertain they had no such knowledge or expectation. Indeed, I have found that those who are acquainted with the procedure and its effects are more difficult to hypnotize and some resist entirely. Moreover, I shall quote a series of most extraordinary results in specially gifted subjects, which were obtained free from any suggestion, every precaution having been taken by myself and the witnesses present to exclude such possibility.

Suggestion implies an involuntary or automatic obedience of the person to the idea which has been presented to him. The subject cannot resist it, even if he should have the desire to do so, and he obeys it as the effect of an abnormal credulity or docility. No doubt there are weak-minded individuals who can be made to do almost anything. We have seen them in the degrading exhibitions by "professors" of hypnotism which used to be common years ago. That is not the kind of hypnotism with which modern medicine and psychology are concerned. It is as

different from it as the methods of the various healing cults are from scientific psychotherapy.

Braid (1843) coined the word *hypnotism* because he saw a similarity between the mesmeric state and sleep; but Mesmer himself and his disciples used the term *animal magnetism* for the same order of facts, and supplied thereby an explanation which did not appeal to the scientists, who rejected the facts together with the theory. Braid in his own time was no more successful. Not until Bernheim was hypnotism as a means of treatment recognized by the medical profession. Bernheim held hypnosis to be all *suggestion*, and nothing but suggestion; thus advancing a theory which does not explain all the facts. Increased suggestibility is a consequence of, but not the cause of, the phenomena produced. Nearly all modern hypnotists are followers of Bernheim. If they had not this preconceived idea that the subject must sleep, and would not impose it upon him, or cause him to inculcate the idea on himself, most of the phenomena called hypnotic could just as well be produced in the waking state.

The hypnotic state, it will be shown presently, is largely a condition of more or less profound *abstraction*. The attention, which in the full waking state is divided by the sense organs and through them by all the impressions received from the external world, is concentrated on a single object and all thought held in abeyance. In this respect the hypnotic state resembles the state of ecstasy. In both there is self-absorption, muscular inactivity, and insensibility to bodily sensations. In both states the person ignores all external objects and takes no account of the lapse of time. Both strengthen the activity of the senses in the direction desired by a flowing together of all that energy which is usually divided between the different sensations. The visions of ecstatics may become realities to their minds; the same as the visions suggested to persons in a state of hypnosis.

The hypnotized person may also be compared to a man engrossed in a play. He is perfectly conscious, and yet in a sense he is hypnotized. One might also compare the consciousness of a hypnotized person with that, say, of a business man who does not think all day of his home, and when at home may not give a single thought to his business; but he is conscious all the time. There is, however, in the hypnotized person a more definite division between his state and the waking state. This will be made clearer to the reader when we deal with the exalted mental powers produced in hypnosis.

The subconscious actions of a hypnotized subject may be compared to those of an absent-minded person, who, though wide-awake, will yet do things with an apparent purpose while not really knowing what he is doing.

Absent-mindedness in a normal person is a spontaneous phenomenon; in hypnosis it is artificially produced. Absent-mindedness is a temporary mental dissociation of a normal kind and terminates suddenly, whether we will or not; whereas hypnosis can be indefinitely protracted by the operator until a suggestion is given to awaken. Because of this resemblance the hypnotic state has been described as a state of dissociation. This is not quite correct, for dissociation in hypnosis is produced only when tricks or tests are practised—that is to say, when things are suggested that are not natural to the subject. When hypnosis is light and restricted to proper therapy it is strictly in accordance with the personality and the desires of the subject, and there is no dissociation, at least no pathological dissociation. There is, therefore, no ground for protest. What such objectors have in their mind is the pathological variety of which they saw so much in the recent war; but the shell-shocked patients, whom they saw and treated, were already dissociated from other causes.

Freud believes that the effects of hypnosis are due to the affection which the subject feels for the operator. McDougall traces the readiness of the subject to accept orders to his being thrust into a state of self-abasement. *With our present knowledge of mental processes it would be best to keep to the facts observed and not indulge too much in theories.* There can be no question that in hypnosis we have to do with a supernormal concentration of attention on one object or subject, with complete unconsciousness of the rest of the external world and of all other sensations. The hypnotic state is a special one, as distinct from the waking state as that is from sleep. There exists a peculiar condition of consciousness which has a specific therapeutic action upon the organism. In hypnosis a person becomes capable of influencing all his bodily functions, increasing or delaying their activity, producing anæsthesia or hyperæsthesia as desired, and having his muscular forces increased or lessened at will. It will be shown that all the senses and mental powers are exalted or can be so enhanced that works are produced which the subject could not accomplish in the normal waking state, and that this exalted activity of the mental powers can be rendered permanent to the great advantage of the subject without any further hypnotic practices. They become part of the subject's natural gifts and personality.

We have to continue to use the term "hypnosis" until a better one is invented. But it is my conviction that the phenomena induced are not due to any special procedure, called hypnotic for the present, but are due to some inherent capacity which varies with different subjects. They are produced by the subject himself, exercising his own powers under the direction of the operator, who does not force his will upon the subject, as many people believe; indeed, the operator does not know how they come about.

The effect of hypnotic influence depends on the fact that the mind of man is largely subconscious, and that this subconscious store of ancestral and individual experience, and of inherited instincts and emotions, can be reached by certain procedures. The subconscious mind supplies the stimulus to thought and action. That is why mere persuasion in the conscious state often fails, for words themselves possess no magic power. Their effect depends on the feelings they arouse. Few men are convinced by logical argument, but their feelings are changed by one who can appeal to their emotions and instincts. If the operator has a knowledge of the world and human nature and speaks with conviction, he can induce the subject to feel and think in unison with him, and since the idea conveyed really corresponds to the subject's own inclination and desire, it will be accepted and acted upon by him as if it originated within himself.

The spontaneous cures of bodily disorders, of which we shall give numerous examples, are also effected by the subconscious mind being accessible in hypnosis. The subconscious mind keeps the wonderful and extraordinarily complicated mechanism of the body in working order, as we have already explained, largely through the sympathetic nervous system which connects the brain with the various bodily organs, and which seems to dominate the life-force. Now, since during hypnosis the conscious mind is in abeyance, the value of hypnotism lies in the fact that it opens a direct road by which suggestion may reach its sphere of action without passing through the conscious mind.

The methods of reaching the subconscious mind will be described in the succeeding chapter. But the good results of hypnosis do not depend on such preliminary procedures, which vary a great deal, but on making the right appeal and suggestion to the subject, who, in most cases, has already made many futile attempts to regain his former mental or bodily state by his own conscious efforts.

CHAPTER IV

METHODS OF HYPNOSIS

In order to bring about hypnosis and influence a subject therapeutically, the most important thing, as I have mentioned in Chapter III, is to create the right emotional atmosphere. The more feeling we can throw into our words, actions, and manner, the greater will be their influence. Only words that come from the heart can reach the heart.

We want to carry conviction, and conviction depends far more upon the trend of the emotions than it does on intellectual endowment. If a person is in an emotional state, and some suggestion is made, or some story told that harmonizes with his emotion, he will generally believe it. It is the same when an orator conveys his emotions to his audience. It matters little what his arguments are; if he cannot inspire, or if he inspires with the wrong emotions, the most perfect chain of reasoning will leave his audience unmoved or hostile. "In all social reactions, it is the emotional factor that counts, not the ideas that are expressed. It is not possible to make a man do what he does not wish to do; but it is quite possible to create an atmosphere in which he does wish to do it, and therefore does it." (Hugh Elliot, *Human Character*.)

In order to make a successful suggestion, we must have the right judgment of the psychic condition of the person to be influenced. In no other branch of therapeutics is it so necessary to individualize and to adapt one's methods to the idiosyncrasies of the patient, his individual qualities, constitution, temper, disposition, and the mood in which he happens to be at the time. We must take note of the patient's intelligence and character, prejudices and beliefs, preferences and dislikes, family life and social surroundings, ambition and prospects, sincerity and energy, memories and fancies, experiences and habits. Therefore, to practise this method of treatment, one must be an expert in human character and possess a knowledge of human nature and practical psychology, besides being gifted with unusual tact and sympathy.

To acquaint ourselves with the mind and character of the subject is our preliminary duty. The best method is undoubtedly to encourage the patient to tell his own story in his own way, with just so much of direction from the physician as will prevent the introduction of too many irrelevancies and trivialities in detail. In this way one gets hold of the material upon which psychotherapy has to operate, and at the same time receives some valuable sidelights upon the relative emphasis that things have assumed in the patient's mind. Furthermore, the sympathetic attention which the physician lends to the initial confession is sure to be rewarded in the future with confidences more intimate and important.

The patient will benefit from the opportunity to unburden his mind to a sympathetic listener; and his confidence in the ability of the physician to help him out of his misery has curative power. Having been enlightened by the physician as to the real nature of his case, understanding his own symptoms, and having further been led to a full belief in the possibility of their removal, the patient advances more easily along the path to recovery.

After these preliminaries we can proceed in the attempt to induce hypnosis. As already indicated, *we are not aiming at getting the subject to sleep*, but to produce such intense concentration and abstraction that the subject becomes unaware of his surroundings; that is to say, pays no voluntary attention to his environment, and even forgets that he has a body and limbs. His senses are quiescent, except for the direction one or other is given by the operator to concentrate the attention. The state produced is identical with that of complete absent-mindedness, as when an ordinary person is meditating deeply and does not notice his sensations. We are indeed aiming at a similar condition for the treatment of disease or disorder, and, as will be shown presently, for the production of supernormal mental capacities.

The room in which the patient is treated should be quiet, in semi-darkness, and contain nothing which captivates the attention too much. The patient being on a couch or in a lounge chair, with a comfortable rest for his head, the first step is to induce in him a mental state of calm and relaxation and to obtain a placid, easy frame of mind. The patient should breathe deeply and regularly, and think of nothing in particular. To prevent distracting ideas arising or his eyes wandering round the room, we get him to fix his gaze, without effort or strain, quite calmly, upon the globe of a lamp, or upon some bright and shining object. He is instructed not to try to keep his eyes open, and not to close them voluntarily, merely to let the lids go as they will. After that, the operator will do well not to speak at all. If the subject shows signs of uneasiness or does not concentrate properly on the object before him, he should, however, be addressed in a gentle and sympathetic tone and calmly reassured.

After a few minutes it will be found that the subject has difficulty in keeping his eyes open, and after some blinking he may close them altogether. Even if his eyes are still open and fixed, his optic nerve will now be tired sufficiently and he may be asked to close his eyes. He is then made to listen to a monotonous sound, such as the ticking of a clock or a metronome. I use an electric motor for the purpose, which can be adjusted to a high or low pitch. The subject is asked to concentrate upon the sound as well as he can, and not to think voluntarily of anything else.

This "power of repose" is closely akin to "mental control," which is the art of preventing our thoughts from being occupied with undesirable matters. He who is able to suspend thought, or to fix his mind on one insignificant thought, will probably have the power also of changing the current of his thoughts at will. The patient generally feels a marked degree of tranquillity, and evinces considerable disinclination to be withdrawn from it. This state of quietude is most agreeable. If we now ask the patient to close his eyelids, they remain closed, as if he had lost all power to open them. His limbs will feel heavy to him and remain motionless in whatever attitude they are in. He has no desire to move. The patient knows he is awake, yet when asked of what he is thinking, he will answer "Nothing."

Persons not used to concentrating may find it difficult to carry out these instructions, in which case they may be asked to concentrate as well as is within their power, and since their mind is wandering off, to let it wander, only not on thoughts connected with their condition and surroundings, but to think of things far away, scenes of their early childhood, of their travels or anything else not connected with the room they are in.

If the patient is fairly passive, we can increase his receptivity by making passes over his face and arms at a distance of about six inches, without directing the subject's attention to them. He is sure to watch them intently, and the sensation they convey, which the old mesmerists thought was due to a magnetic fluid, will bring him into closer mental contact with the operator.

Still another method is to stroke gently the subject's forehead or one of his hands. This, besides calming his excitability, makes him forget any pain that he may previously have felt, and concentrates his attention.

By all these methods we secure a limitation of the field of consciousness, a state of absent-mindedness. The subject becomes unconscious of his surroundings, and his subconscious mind is liberated.

Most modern hypnotists practise the Nancy method, i.e. suggesting to the patient the effects they wish to produce: that he is getting drowsy, his eyelids begin to feel heavy, he has a difficulty in raising them and will soon not be able to lift them at all, and so forth. But, in my experience, if the hypnotist speaks too much, the patient expects, waits for, and relies on the suggestions made, a result which is not desirable, for it makes the subject too dependent on the operator.

The old mesmerists compelled their subjects to look steadily at their eyes while they gazed at them firmly. They then made slow passes with one or both hands downwards from the crown of the patient's head over the face to the pit of the stomach, or even down to the feet, always avoiding contact. After each pass the hands were well shaken, just as if something were shaken off them. The passes would be continued patiently for some time, until they excited the sensation of warmth, pricking or tingling, numbness or rigidity, according to the individual operated upon. By another method, the magnetizer would sit down close to the patient, taking hold of his thumbs, and gently pressing them gaze fixedly in his eyes, concentrating his mind upon him, while the subject would gaze at the operator. The gaze of the subject had the effect of concentrating the subject's attention, and the look of the operator, as it were, commanded him not to "wander" in his thoughts. The old magnetizers laid the greatest stress on the intense concentration on the part of the operator, and would often achieve success solely by intent gazing, without passes or verbal suggestion. In my experience, however, the gazing process cannot be employed by everyone. It requires a sharp, penetrating look, capable of long-continued fixedness; it will likewise seldom succeed with individuals who are magnetized for the first time.

The magnetizers, finding the patients not yielding to the influence of their passes, would close their eyes and press the fingers gently on the eyelids and retain them there for a few minutes, at the same time concentrating all their efforts.

Another method was to hold two fingers before the subject's eyes and ask him to gaze at their tips, and to concentrate his attention on the idea of sleep. The fingers were moved from a distance close to the eyes and away again, when the tiring effect of constant accommodation of vision often produced the desired effect.

At public performances magnetizers used soft strains of music, issuing from an adjoining room, which lulled the subjects and appeared to assist greatly the induction of sleep in new subjects.

These mesmeric methods are more suitable for the deeper states of hypnosis, the trance-like conditions, in which the limbs remain in the position in which they are put. If the hands are clasped together, the subject cannot get them apart; or, if he is made to rotate his arms, he cannot stop the movement until the hypnotist tells him he can do so. These deep states are not really required except as tests, or when dealing with very severe symptoms, or when we study certain phenomena of hypnosis in subjects who volunteer for scientific purposes. For such deep hypnosis not all persons are suitable, because they lack the required susceptibility or because, though they are consciously willing, they subconsciously resist.

Still, any of these methods may be tried, and sometimes must be, for some persons are more impressionable to one method than to another. Some are distracted when touched, while others go off more easily when they feel the contact of the operator. As a matter of fact, all processes succeed when they inspire confidence in the subject.

As a rule, each hypnotizer has his own pet method, but the expert is able to judge the mental susceptibility of the subject at first sight, and can tell at once what process would be most successful.

A good preliminary test whether a person can be hypnotized is to judge his sensibility by drawing the palm of the hand downwards, without contact, but very near, over his face and hands. This is best done while the eyes are closed, when it will be found that some subjects have a peculiar sensation, varying from mere warmth to pricking, and, in the most susceptible, as if a mild electric current passed over their skin. This used to be described by mesmerists as the magnetic influence, and although no such influence is admitted now, I have always found that these passes were felt more readily and by more persons when I had been doing much hypnotic work than when I had rested for some time.

For medical purposes we need only aim at the early stage preceding sleep that is consistent with consciousness. This is the transitional stage which anyone who has analysed his sensations has recognized as a brief period immediately preceding the unconsciousness of slumber, when by an effort he can become wide awake, or by lying still and guarding his mind against exciting thoughts can insure speedy and perfect sleep.

The induction of this semi-wakeful state is, as a rule, all that is needed, and is a fairly simple process. And in all cases hypnosis is more readily induced for medical treatment than for any other purpose, because in the sick the voluntary and conscious activity is diminished by exhaustion, and the subjects are really earnest about it in order to be cured. But it is not only sick people, or people suffering from nervous or other disorders, that can be hypnotized; perfectly healthy people make equally excellent subjects. Nor has the weakness of "will" anything to do with the susceptibility of a subject. What sometimes hinders hypnotization is "mental pre-occupation," which, however, may suddenly at some moment be removed. Nor are "credulous" persons necessarily good subjects. There are plenty of people who believe all they are told, yet often offer a lively resistance when an effort is made to hypnotize them.

Insane people are notoriously hard to hypnotize, because of the difficulty of engaging their attention and getting them to concentrate. But with persons in the primary stages of mental disorder—that is to say, not altogether mad—there is no such difficulty.

It will be noticed that, though all the methods we have described for inducing hypnosis vary, the conditions are practically the same:

1. First and foremost is that of fixation of the attention.
2. Monotonous environment, to produce monotonous impressions and intellectual drowsiness, the prelude of sleep.
3. Limitation of voluntary movements by relaxation of the muscles.
4. Limitation of the field of consciousness by allowing no new incoming impression and
5. Inhibition of ideas by making the mind as nearly as possible a blank.

These conditions suffice for all practical purposes. Sleep need not be induced, but only the somnolent state we have described. This method has the advantage that nearly everybody can be subjected to it.

Most important is the fixation of attention. In the physical procedure it is the sensorial attention that is fixed; when the procedure is purely suggestive, the attention is held captive by an idea. It would seem, then, that a special modification of attention is a persistent psychological characteristic of hypnosis.

We can now address the subject, speak plainly and emphatically to him about his ailment or injurious habit, and he will remain perfectly passive, so long as we say nothing with which he is likely to disagree. If the idea runs counter to the sentiments and firmly held beliefs of the individual, other things being equal, he is much less likely to accept it than if it accords with his own feelings and convictions.

In the case of minor mental disorders and over-active dispositions, we can impress upon him the desire to break himself of the morbid idea or impulse, and, by calling his own powers of thought and volition into play, we can show him the way to self-control.

The manner in which an idea is conveyed is often the determining factor in the patient's suggestibility regarding it. It may be presented directly or indirectly, persuasively or commandingly, once or repeatedly. The idea may be put forward as an abstract proposition, or crystallized in the form of a picture or a practical demonstration.

It is advisable to condense the idea which is to be the object of the suggestion, to sum it up in a brief phrase which can readily be graven on the memory.

Whatever idea is presented to the mind in hypnotic

treatment is intended as a *post-hypnotic suggestion*, to take effect after waking. When subjects are subsequently questioned as to their motive for acting, they generally believe that they have so acted of their own accord; for no suggestion is made in medical treatment which the patient would not himself desire.

The suggestion made for post-hypnotic action may be direct or indirect. A direct suggestion would be, for example, if we told an alcoholic subject that he will no longer have a desire for drink. This, in many instances, will not work at all, because it does not give the patient a motive for abstaining. I much-prefer giving indirect suggestions, such as will provide him (in the case of the alcoholic) with pictures of utter ruin and degradation if he persists in the habit, and of his success in life, the realization of his aims and ideals, his gaining respect and esteem if he will abstain. This supplies the patient not only with the necessary motives, but also with the *emotional background* so essential for the successful exercise of his will.

If we tell a person in the conscious state that a certain habit is detrimental to his health, he will say that he knows as much, but cannot break himself of it. If we draw attention to his habit, while he is in the concentrated state of hypnosis, and supply him with reasons why he should stop it, he receives the message passively, i.e. subconsciously, and automatically acts upon it. When later he is tempted again, there comes into play a restraining impulse, an inhibition, and sometimes even a repulsion of the former desire.

We shall succeed best by projecting upon the mind of the subject a new and stimulating idea, which will have a wholesome, regenerating, aspiring, uplifting effect. We do not employ, therefore, so much a method of suggestion as is commonly assumed, but we train the patient to act by his own will. Especially where there is a conflict of emotions it is better not to make any suggestions, but to let the patient pass into a state of reverie. This enables the subconscious to break through to the surface, and, by allowing the patient to talk about whatever comes into his mind, we may bring to consciousness an event, long forgotten, which is at the root of all the patient's troubles.

The free talk in the passive, uncritical, subconscious state will reveal not only those "complexes" arising from past events which are still smouldering and exerting an undesirable influence on conscious life and behaviour, and giving rise to physical symptoms, but may also reveal to the operator's critical faculty a failure of adaptation, which he must rectify. So long as the complexes are unconscious they are beyond our control; merely bringing them into consciousness helps to remove the trouble from which the patient is suffering. In any case, having discovered where the mischief lies, we are able to advise the patient and re-educate him to take a proper view of life and to adapt himself to the conditions of his surroundings.

All psychic treatment strives to free the innate forces that have been bound and to adjust the individual to that external reality in which he must live. (P. Bjerre.)

No psychotherapy is any good, certainly not lasting, if it does not include the re-education of the patient; for his illness is often nothing more than an unsuccessful effort to solve the conflicts of his life and a failure of adaptation. We have to bring about a readjustment, some sought-for and desirable reorganization of the individual in respect of his inner and outer experiences, to assist him, as well as may be, in his efforts, hitherto frustrated, toward the consummation of a more harmonious adaptation to his social and physical environment. In other words, we seek the reconciliation of the patient with reality. We evoke new ideals and the impulse to pursue them, and make them so attractive to the patient that they become embodied in the processes of his conduct. Of course, the ideals must be practical, not Utopian. By the implanting of new ideals we tap the potential subconscious reserve energy of the patient, bring about a reassociation and synthesis of the dissociated mental systems underlying the symptoms of the disease, and guide the mind of the patient to self-realization and self-perfection. The subject must be brought to realize his previous misconceptions, his undesirable mental habits have to be uprooted, he must be taught to minimize his difficulties, to stop the magnification of trifles, and to gain self-control. We have to teach him orderly thought and controlled emotion, and supply him with new motives for right conduct. Undesirable elements of mental life have to be supplanted by the concentration of attention on new interests, the furnishing of new outlets of activities. A new attitude and outlook on life has to be acquired and disturbing inner or outer conditions have to be adjusted. *Mere exploration of his mental contents without such re-education is bound to prove a failure.*

By the methods I have described, the subject retains his consciousness unimpaired, and can, if requested, discuss and reason with the operator or any person present with more intelligence than before. It will be found that the concentration he practised while on the couch or in the chair has increased the energy and power of his ideas, so that he will have more determination for the realization of his aims. Again I lay stress, there must be an emotional contact between the subject and operator. Men of sympathetic personality will always have more influence than those of a colder nature. The cold, commanding personality succeeds, if at all, chiefly by the fear he inspires.

We have seen that the factors necessary for successful mental healing are, first of all, sympathy for the sufferer, which must be expressed in gentle words and action, to bring peace to his mind and bodily activity. Then hope with which to reanimate the reserves of energy. Stimulating words revive the faith and induce the patient to make an effort. They encourage him to gain control, to keep alive. Furthermore, we have to take stock of the patient's mind and assess its various contents at their proper value.

In all diseases, whether functional or organic, there is a psychical factor, for man does not suffer like an animal, feeling only crude sensations, but his feelings are influenced by his fears and pessimistic reflections, and often his mental suffering is greater than the actual bodily pain. We have to deal not merely with the symptoms as they present themselves to the patient's consciousness, but with the interpretation he invariably places upon these symptoms.

On the other hand, actual pain, though we can remove it in hypnosis, must be traced to its causes; for all pain that is not imaginary is a signal of some disorder or disease, which, if unattended, is bound to increase. To remove pain without discovering its cause is a dangerous proceeding.

Last, but not least, *the physical needs of the patient must not be neglected.* We must not lose sight of the fact that disease has a physical basis, and that even in functional affections there is some nutritional or other disturbance, some change in the bio-chemistry of the tissues, which cannot be corrected by merely making suggestions to the patient. We must restore not merely the mental condition, but the health of the organization with which mind is connected, and upon the normal state of which its soundness depends. Much good can be accomplished by psychical measures, but those who are not carried away by enthusiasm will recognize that psychotherapy is not a panacea, and, although valuable in many cases, should not be employed to the exclusion of other measures. It is the duty of the practitioner when called upon to treat a patient to carry out not one, but all of the measures which have been shown by years of experience to be advantageous. He therefore requires an intimate knowledge of the normal working and the disorders of the brain and nervous system, and a proper knowledge of general medicine. These qualifications only a properly trained physician can possess.

The first thing to do is to put the patient on the best physical basis. Then we have solved part of the problem of his mental condition. We examine his constitution to discover any defect there may be in the working of an organ, and treat such defect according to the recognized methods of medical science. We do not, as Christian Scientists and practitioners of other cults do, relegate tried methods to the dust-heap, but recognize that, even if there be no actual disease anywhere about the body, the patient, owing to his habitual indulgence in morbid thoughts or habits, has weakened his constitution, and may suffer from a state of nervous exhaustion or irritability, which requires our treatment on established lines.

CHAPTER V

THE APPLICATION OF HYPNOTISM TO THE TREATMENT OF BODILY AND MENTAL DISORDERS

RAPID and lasting cures can be achieved by hypnotic treatment. No other treatment, certainly no other form of psychotherapy, can produce such results.

First of all, as regards physiological effects produced in hypnosis, the *pulse* can be quickened or retarded, *respiration* slowed or accelerated, and *perspiration* can be produced, if needed. Even the *temperature* can be affected. A healthy *appetite* can be created, the action of the bowels regulated, and, what is more remarkable, the *menstrual period* in ordinary amenorrhœa can be determined to the day and hour.

Insomnia is most readily treated by hypnosis, even when accompanied by painful sensations, and when all medical remedies have failed. As a matter of fact, it is only then, as a rule, that the possibility of relief by hypnosis is thought of.

One of the most sensational spontaneous recoveries in my experience was that of a young girl who had arrived from India seriously ill with constant vomiting and persistent insomnia. Two eminent physicians had treated her in a nursing home with antitoxins, without result. As she gradually got worse and lost weight rapidly, it occurred to them that the cause of her trouble might be mental, and I was sent for. I did not attempt a long course of psycho-analysis, but tested her for hypnosis. She proved a good subject and I elicited from her a confession which completely accounted for her symptoms; though in her ordinary state she denied that she had any mental trouble whatever. She slept the same night and every succeeding night seven and a half hours, and the vomiting ceased the first morning and did not return. The patient had gained half a stone in weight at the end of a week when she left the home.

By hypnotic treatment we can relieve most forms of *pain*, including headache, migraine, ear-ache, and even pain after surgical operations. To relate one history only: that of a boy who had been run over by a trolley, which smashed his ankle. After operation the patient had so much pain in the joint that he could not sleep, and the surgeon thinking that possibly a nerve had been involved in the healing process, again opened up the wound, but to no effect. After the usual medicinal remedies had been tried by mouth and by injection, hypnosis was suggested. The boy was a most difficult subject, and I nearly despaired of succeeding. Then I must have hit upon the right suggestion to influence this sceptical youth, for his pain disappeared and he slept soundly that night, and every following night, and after a few days more rest he came to see me, completely recovered.

Another difficult case was recommended by an

Oxford doctor. It was a man suffering from *facial neuralgia* for five years, who had undergone a variety of treatments without benefit. He was hypnotized and made a spontaneous recovery, and there was no return for years after, as I have been able to ascertain.

As regards *headache*, it is very important to discover the origin of the complaint, for it may be due to physical disorders or arise from emotional causes alone. In some people duties which they do not like to undertake, or events which they anticipate with anxiety, are apt to bring on the pain. I know a woman who suffered from headache whenever her husband, for whom she had no love, asked her to go out with him; and another, who was very happy in her matrimonial life, but had been allowed in early childhood to complain of pains and sickness whenever she did not want to go to school or do anything else that was disagreeable to her.

Treatment by hypnotism may be successfully employed in *chorea*, *muscular tremors*, *and nervous tics*. I had one case which resembled so much the sudden recoveries claimed for Lourdes that I should like to give its history. A girl, age 22, was sent to me by a doctor in Fulham. She had suffered for ten years from chorea, the sequela of rheumatic fever and heart complications (endocarditis). She had lost the power over her lower limbs and was brought to me in a Bath-chair. She also suffered from insomnia and night terrors. At the second interview hypnotism was attempted and repeated several times at intervals, with the result best given in the words of her sister, who wrote to me:

After leaving your house on Friday we walked along Oxford Street, through the lower department of Selfridge's, on to Marble Arch, and across the Park to St. George's Hospital, where we took an omnibus for home; that, for a girl who has scarcely walked a yard and has been wheeled about in a Bath-chair since two years ago last May, is little less than a miracle. She is sleeping splendidly and naturally. All her terrible night fears have ceased to trouble her—and us. Her screams used to rouse us all at times. Her new cheery outlook on things in general would be laughable if we were not so intensely thankful. It seems almost impossible—a fortnight ago an apparently incurable invalid, again and again unconscious in her Bath-chair in the streets, and now to-day, and every day since your treatment began, a normal, cheerful girl who is able to move about and speak, and whom it is a pleasure to be with.

Some years have elapsed since then, but when I saw the doctor recently he assured me that the patient was now a fine woman and had kept perfectly well.

Another medical practitioner brought me a lady suffering from neck and shoulder *spasms*, whom I did not think I could treat by hypnotism, for she could not keep still on the couch. In this case I had to use a sedative by way of preliminary treatment, after which hypnosis was made possible, and she, too, made a perfect recovery.

Inco-ordination of muscular movement and tremors occur most often in people suffering from a sense of inferiority. They lack self-confidence and self-assertion, and frequently they are morbidly shy and self-conscious. An inferiority complex is often the primary cause of the inco-ordination of another set of muscles, those involved in speech, giving rise to *stuttering* and *stammering*. Many cases have been treated by me. The method I follow is after induction of hypnosis to remove first of all the anxiety about speech. Training of the voice is very good, but insufficient without this preliminary. Exercises are curative chiefly by inspiring confidence, but they take time; whereas by hypnosis we can remove the fear of speech and the sense of inferiority at once. That stammering is not a mere disorder of speech is shown by the fact that the patient can usually speak perfectly when alone or amongst his intimates, and fails only amongst strangers. That is why he avoids company and inclines towards solitude.

The stammerers that present difficulty are those who are constitutionally defective and lack nervous energy. For this reason I test them before commencing treatment. Thus, one day I had two stammerers to treat. One a boy of fourteen, and another four years of age. I asked the former to put his foot down and say: I must speak properly. He gently touched the floor with his foot and stammered in a low tone the words I told him. I knew by this he would take some time to recover. The other boy I asked also to put his foot down and say: I am going to be a great orator. This boy stamped the floor and carefully, in slow but emphatic tones, he said: "Indeed, I am not going to be an orator, I am going to be an engineer." He was well within a week.

Another disorder, for which the hypnotist is frequently consulted, is *occupational cramp*, which affects writers, violinists, and others who have to use their fingers to excess, until fatigue supervenes. This disability, at its first occurrence, may be accidental, consequent upon some overstressed effort. However, in a person over-anxious, the failure causes a fear of future failure, which interferes with the harmonious automatism. It is the effort to overcome this which produces and perpetuates the cramp. By hypnosis we can remove the anxiety, and so remove the effect.

Epilepsy is a disease not usually treated by hypnotism; but when it arises from psychical causes the emotional state associated with the disturbance of consciousness may be influenced in hypnosis and the patient trained to take heed of warnings so as to prevent an attack.

Then there are such varied troubles as noises in the ear, spasmodic asthma, and hyperthyroidism which can be relieved in hypnosis. In the last disorder, which may arise from sudden shock, I have seen the heart going at a furious speed, with excessive emotionalism, tremor of the hands, insomnia, and yet the mental and physical state became completely restored.

Incontinence of urine is a frequent complaint among children. I have had a number of adults as well with the same weakness, and treated them successfully by hypnotism. Most of them suffered from nocturnal bed-wetting; but I had one case of a girl with claustrophobia, who, when in church, a theatre, or hall, had to rush out to relieve herself. Another girl, age 21, still had persistent incontinence, and her brother, a doctor, had sought all possible advice to relieve her. Finally, he thought of hypnosis. She made an immediate recovery, and I am told she is now happily married and the mother of several children. Another case was that of a young teacher, who felt keenly his weakness as he had little boys under him with the same complaint. He, too, made a quick recovery and continued well.

It is often denied that *organic disease*—disease which causes a permanent and often progressive organic change in the tissues—as distinguished from functional disorder, can be benefited by hypnotic treatment. We must not forget that there is a mental element in all diseases and that the nervous system is implicated, and in so far as we can influence it for good we can minimize the disease. No one would claim thus to make lame men walk; yet I have seen them make successful efforts in hypnosis. That does not say that their paralysis was cured. Their legs were still paralysed, but evidently they could in this state recollect the co-ordination of movement of former times and had greater power over their muscles, enabling them to make better use of their paralysed limbs.

If in organic diseases we can procure sleep and

abolish pain, there is a much better chance of recovery. Even if the disease be incurable we can at least make the remaining months or years of life tolerable for the patient. The sick person is more emotional and suggestible. The man who feels sure of getting well eats better and sleeps better. The very action of the heart is promoted by this hopeful and contented attitude of the mind.

That sleep can be induced must be acknowledged, but so also can pain be abolished, no matter whether the hypnosis is the work of others or self-induced. Thus the martyrs of old who suffered death by torture were probably in a mental state of self-hypnosis. Their mind was so absorbed with the single idea of the cause for which they were dying that, as in hypnosis, physical sensations failed to reach their consciousness. Warriors, too, in the heat of battle, often fail to notice the wounds they have received. And mighty men of genius have completed their life-work in face of a painful disease which before long claimed its victim.

Again I am in a position to relate an extraordinary case, that of a woman lying ill with cancer in a nursing home. The surgeon had done his utmost to make her sleep, but notwithstanding all remedies the constant spasms of pain kept her awake, and she was slowly sinking. The patient went under hypnotic influence almost immediately and she slept, but only about three minutes, when with a sudden start of pain she woke again. I continued my attempts; finally, after an hour, by gently stroking the patient's arms and hands, I got her to sleep peacefully. A week later I received a letter of thanks from the mother acknowledging that the patient had slept well every night after and kept free from pain.

I have often applied hypnotism successfully to patients about to undergo surgical operation and unduly excited about it, or refusing to submit to it. We can bring about physical and mental repose, establish equanimity, and prevent the excessive anxiety associated with the operation, or with the taking of an anæsthetic. Shock is diminished, and the patients awake from the narcosis as if they had been merely asleep.

Just prior to the discovery of chloroform many surgical operations were painlessly performed upon mesmerized patients (*Numerous Cases of Surgical Operations without pain in the Mesmeric State*, by John Elliotson, M.D., F.R.S., London, 1843). James Esdaile, a Medical Officer of the East India Company, who used mesmerism for the production of anæsthesia in surgical operations, was so successful that a small hospital was granted him in Calcutta in 1846, where he performed many major and a multitude of minor surgical operations on mesmerized patients. (*Mesmerism in India*, 1846.)

Every hypnotist gets a large number of sufferers from *morbid fears*. These are of various kinds. Some people fear open spaces (agoraphobia) and refuse to go out by themselves into streets or anywhere in the open. Others fear closed places (claustrophobia) and cannot go to a theatre or hall, or cannot travel by omnibus or train, or if they do, they are panic-struck when travelling alone in a compartment; others cannot enter an occupied compartment. Some people fear objects, such as knives; others fear living things, such as cats or other animals. Some fear the elements, waters, rivers, sea, thunder, lightning, darkness. Some fear functions as respiration, swallowing, blushing, writing. Some again fear diseases, especially heart-disease and insanity. Others fear self-destruction, premature death, or sudden collapse. It is not ordinary fear that they experience, but excess of fear, amounting to terror, and they exhibit all the symptoms of it. The heart-beat is quickened, they may shiver or perspire, and some of them faint when brought into contact with the object of their fear. These fears are unreasonable, but the subject is unable to drive them away. The attempt to do so makes them feel worse and they therefore avoid the situations which give rise to their particular fears.

Patients suffering from morbid fears hardly ever recover spontaneously in hypnosis, and often offer considerable resistance to the operator. The reason is that they are self-hypnotized, and we have to break the spell. Let us take, for example, a person with agoraphobia. He refuses to go out into the open by himself, declaring that he experiences a sensation as if the houses were tumbling upon him. He feels faint and suffers the greatest agony. No reasoning will avail. He behaves exactly the same as if these things had been suggested to him in deep hypnosis. He is self-hypnotized. His emotional disturbances are genuine. Through the sympathetic nervous system one or other bodily function becomes abnormally active, producing the sensation of dying.

Whereas Freud, the founder of the modern psychoanalytic school, finds in all these cases some derangement of the sex functions, this, in my experience, is true only of some cases. Nearly all patients suffer from a sense of inferiority (Adler). In a number the fear can be traced back to some fear-inspiring incident in childhood or early youth, which has been ill-repressed. In all of them we have to unravel the complex which interferes with their proper conduct, we have to bring the cause of their anxiety—the original emotional experience—before their consciousness and under control and censorship, and have to re-educate them to adapt themselves to the circumstances of life. We have to give them new interests, so as to keep them fully occupied, for occupation employs the intellect and keeps the emotions inactive. Altogether they must be helped by a sympathetic and philosophic understanding.

By far the largest number of patients who seek help from the hypnotist are people addicted to *bad habits*, whether to alcohol, drugs, self-abuse, or other perverse sex practices. Here the habit is often so deeply ingrained that quick results are the exception. Perverse habits undermine the physical health and destroy the mental energy and will power. Their treatment requires the co-operation of the patient.

He must be willing to make an effort, and this is just what he is not able or willing to do. He would like to see a miracle performed, to go to sleep and wake up a changed being. Such cures are sometimes achieved, but they do not happen every day. If they did, they would cease to be miraculous. That instantaneous cures do sometimes take place, the following cases will prove.

One case is that of a lady over sixty years of age, a habitual drunkard, brought to me by a physician in Putney, who himself had considerable experience in hypnosis and who made it a condition to be present during the treatment. She was deeply hypnotized at the first sitting, and taught to look with disgust on her former vice, and to find pleasure in natural and healthy modes of life. She came twice more at intervals of a week, and the doctor assured me, when I saw him later, that this lady had kept to total abstinence ever since.

Another instance of spontaneous recovery is that of a drug-taker (morphia injections), who could not for a long time make up his mind to submit to treatment. When he ultimately came, he, too, made a good subject. On the second day he brought me all his stock of morphia and syringes, and he has never fallen back since, as confirmed by his wife, and acknowledged by himself in affectionate letters every New Year.

Still another case was that of perverse sexual practices by a man of some distinction, who might have risen higher in his profession had he not lowered his vitality by his terrible addiction. He, too, was successfully treated, though it took some time before he completely recovered. There can be no greater acknowledgment of the value of psycho-therapy than was conveyed by this patient in a letter to me in which he said: "You are to me a Solomon of wisdom and a mountain of moral strength."

The nervous and emotional disorders known under the collective term *hysteria* have always formed a big field for hypnotic treatment. Sometimes they are due to painful emotional experiences, which have not been successfully banished from the mind and continue subconsciously to influence the patient's feelings and conduct. By the searchlight of psycho-analysis, or more quickly by hypnosis, the cause of the emotional disturbance is revealed and can be brought before the patient's consciousness. Sometimes the hysterical symptoms are manifestations or expressions of unconscious, unfulfilled wishes and have to be recognized by the patient. Sometimes they are due to faulty upbringing, or to external circumstances which conflict with the patient's longings and notions of life.

Most hysterical symptoms seem to arise from self-hypnosis. There is a narrowing of the field of consciousness, exaggerated absent-mindedness, and increased suggestibility. It is the narrowing of the field of consciousness that makes one set of their ideas all powerful, while others drop out of the field of their perception (amnesia), bodily sensations may not be perceived (anæsthesia), and they may be devoid of the knowledge of how to move their limbs (functional paralysis). What auto-suggestion has caused, hetero-suggestion (suggestion by others) can cure. To prevent relapse we have to combat the increased suggestibility and the emotionalism, and must unify divided states of consciousness—in other words, we must re-educate the patient.

Genuine *mental disorders* are most difficult to treat. As a rule, only the early stages can be benefited. In the more advanced stages of mental derangement, we have to wait for the more or less lucid moments, in which the patient is receptive to other ideas than those which preoccupy him. We have to take care not to arouse his antagonism. In the milder forms of melancholia, we may dissipate the anxiety and fears; in the early stages of paranoia, we may dispel the suspicions; and in dementia præcox, some good may be done and the progress of the disease arrested if the patient still has insight of his mental condition. Treatment of these disorders requires considerable patience and we must proceed cautiously. More promising is the so-called *folie raisonnante* or reasoning mania, in which the patient questions everything, suffers from doubts, mental hesitation, and indecision.

Among the minor mental troubles which can be treated hypnotically are *obsessions*. They consist most often of useless conscious ideas which occupy the mind of the patient to the exclusion of nearly everything else and dominate his character and actions.

In hypnosis we can bring the experiences in which the fixed idea originated before consciousness, and dispel any anxiety connected with them.

Loss of memory, in most cases, can be treated successfully in hypnosis. Only when due to head-injury and subsequent destruction of brain cells is the condition hopeless. Two of the most interesting cases that have come before me were the following. Both were due to concussion of the brain. One was the commander of a submarine boat which had exploded. The patient had not been visibly injured but was unconscious when rescued. He had married a few months before the accident, an incident in his life which, on leaving hospital, he had completely forgotten. In fact, he did not recognize his wife and refused to live with her. The other was a similar case, caused by a railway accident. When I saw the man the first time, he addressed me with the words, "The lady standing by my side says she is my wife, but I have no recollection of having married." In both these cases the memory was successfully restored by hypnosis.

Conscious hypnosis may be applied for purposes of *education*. In a great many cases of youths who have been hypnotized for the relief of some ailment, bad habit, or disorder, the parents have asked me to awaken some slumbering talent or renewed interest in some study or pursuit, and, as will be shown presently, all mental faculties can be raised in power, so that better work is accomplished than had been done before. Quite a large number of young men I have helped over their examinations in such varying subjects as the law, accountancy, engineering, surveying, civil service subjects, military and naval science. Inattentive and forgetful boys have acquired concentration and memory; timidity and weakness will have been turned into self-confidence and decision; and application became easy to them by the very training given during hypnosis.

As regards *moral education*, the entire personal character may be influenced in hypnosis. Quarrelsomeness, over-sensitiveness, obstinacy, and other failings which mar the prospects of a person may be rectified. Some children are positively ungovernable. Some are hopelessly wicked. Here, when the ordinary educational measures have failed, we can bring about changes in character and habits. Weak capacities may be stimulated, a kleptomanic may be restrained, a case of habitual lying may be influenced, evil habits may be uprooted, a mental force and moral sentiment induced, and a useful character developed. Guiding ideas that will produce interest, enthusiasm, and noble passions may be introduced, and high purpose and noble endeavour may be substituted in the character for carnal propensities and sordid aims, worthy ideals for bestial standards, intellectual brillance and living interest for obtuseness and indifference. Habits of thought-concentration may be made to take the place of habits of rambling, nervousness, and timidity. Habitual indolence and disinclination to exertion can be overcome, and a subject may have a real interest excited and motive supplied, which have a bearing on his future activity in the world. Sometimes the deficiency or perverseness is inborn; in others we can trace the cause to upbringing, such as a wrong mental attitude in the spoiled or bullied child, which hinders adjustment in later years.

I have seen social misfits and moral perverts of all kinds, youths addicted to lying, fraud, stealing, and with the obtuseness of feeling of possible murderers. Much depends on the diagnosis, for we cannot help the actual degenerate, and the youth with arrested brain development; but there are many men now occupying honourable positions whose parents at one time sat weeping in my consulting-room. Again I could quote many striking and interesting cases, but naturally must refrain to avoid identification.

CHAPTER VI

ACCENTUATION OF THE SENSES FOLLOWING HYPNOSIS

HYPNOTISM, since it has received general acknowledgment, has been applied chiefly to the treatment of nervous disorders. Consequently, the notion is prevalent that only persons of great excitability, weak-mindedness, or hysterical disposition make good subjects, and that the higher phenomena produced by the old mesmerists must have been due either to suggestion, self-deception, or fraud. Hence I determined to experiment on normal subjects, whose consent I could obtain for the purpose, and test what are the powers manifested in the hypnotic state and immediately on awakening, independent of any conscious, or (so far as I could judge) subconscious suggestion.

The hypnotic state is induced as usual and as soon as the necessary concentration of attention is reached, the person is roused, and the experiments performed, which I am about to relate.

I may state at once that all these experiments have been repeated (without the preliminary hypnosis, which on repetition is no longer necessary) during the past thirty years, before small and large audiences, consisting of learned and scientifically trained men and sometimes entirely of medical experts.

After the first successful performance of the experiment, there is no further need of the operator's presence, and it is my custom to leave the subject entirely to the audience. This does away with the objection that the subject is hardly ever left to his own inspiration but is dependent on the operator for the manifestation of the phenomena. On the contrary, the subject, though he manifests exalted powers, is in his perfectly normal state and able to converse freely with any people present.

In this chapter I shall deal only with the accentuation of the special senses.

Those familiar with the phenomena of hypnosis are familiar with the fact that all the senses in this state are greatly accentuated.

Let us take, first of all, the *sense of sight*. A popular experiment is the following: The operator or any onlooker takes a packet of blank ivory cards, note-paper, or envelopes, fresh from the stationer's, and shows one of these cards or envelopes to the hypnotized subject, who is now awake, afterwards shuffling it in amongst the others, and remembering its position. The pack is then returned to the subject, who as a rule without hesitation picks out the right card or other object from the number handed to him, although no difference is perceptible to the most skilful observer watching the performance.

This experiment, which was first performed by me in 1904 (see *Ethological Journal*, 1905), and has often been repeated since, has more recently been done by Dr. H.

Yellowlees (*Manual of Psychotherapy*, 1923), who acknowledges that the subject's "special senses can be sharpened and intensified by the physician's suggestion to a remarkable degree." For example, the subject "is given an ordinary playing-card, and shown both sides of it, being told that he is to take note of it, and be able to recognize it. The card is then mixed with a dozen others which are finally dealt out before him face downwards. A good subject has no difficulty in picking out this card from among the rest, although the backs appear identical to the ordinary observer. This feat is a particularly striking one, and seems wellnigh incredible; but the writer has had patients perform it on several occasions, and the successes have been more numerous than the failures, although every precaution and safeguard has been taken." Dr. Yellowlees thinks that the patient evidently recognizes the card by minute markings on the back, which are indistinguishable to the ordinary sight, for his most striking failure was in a case "where a perfectly new and unused pack was procured for the test." This explanation cannot be correct, for I have always in my experiments used only new packs of cards that have never been opened, and I have chosen other objects, in their original packing, every time with the same results.

Some experimenters suggest that a photograph should appear on the back of one of the cards, by which illusion the subject invariably recognizes the card. I have often done so, and when the card, quite unintentionally, is handed to the subject upside down, he will remark the same about the photograph. This experiment is no less wonderful, but Moll (*Hypnotism*, 1909) has an adverse explanation for it, which cannot be passed over. He says:

I will take this opportunity of quoting an experiment which is often repeated and is wrongly considered as a proof of increased keenness of the senses. Let us take a pack of cards, which naturally must have backs of the same pattern, so that to all appearances one cannot be distinguished from the other. Let us choose a card—the ace of hearts, for example—hold it with its back to the subject and arouse by suggestion the idea of a particular photograph on it—his own, let us say. Let us shuffle the cards, including, of course, that with the supposed photograph on it, and request the hypnotic to find the photograph, without having allowed him to see the face of the cards. He will often find the right one, although the backs are alike. The experiment can be repeated with visiting-cards, or with sheets of paper, if the selected one is marked, unknown to the hypnotic. This experiment makes a greater impression on the inexperienced than it is entitled to, for most people are able to repeat the experiment without hypnosis, and hyperæsthesia is not generally a condition for its success. If the back of these cards and papers are carefully examined, differences which may easily be discerned will be discovered. The experiment has no bearing on the question of simulation. Naturally, I do not contend that a hypnotic cannot find a paper in such a case better than a waking man. I only wish to point out that although this experiment is often used to demonstrate the presence of hyperæsthesia, the latter is not generally necessary for its success. I have seen men of science show astonishment when a hypnotic distinguished apparently identical sheets of paper. They did not understand that there were essential differences in the sheets, which suffice for distinguishing them even without hypnosis. The experiment is to be explained thus: The minute but recognizable difference (*points de repère*) presented to the hypnotic at the moment when the idea of the photograph was suggested to him, recall the suggested image directly he sees them again. The points are so closely associated with the image that they readily call it up. Binet and Féré have rightly pointed out that the image only occurs when the *points de repère* are recalled to the memory; they must first be seen. Consequently, if the paper is held at a distance from the subject's eyes, the image will not be recognized, for the *points de repère* are not visible.

I absolutely deny that a normal person can distinguish a blank card out of a pack of identical cards owing to any defect or peculiarity in the manufacture, if the same conditions are followed that I have made obligatory in my experiments. Only one card out of an unused pack is shown to the subject, which is shuffled by some stranger, who must remember whether it is the fifth or fifteenth or any other card, but who need not remain in the room, so as to avoid any suspicion of thought transference. Nor, of course, should anyone else know, least of all the operator. The subject, on receiving the pack, will take up one card after another and as soon as arriving at the right one will stop, without looking at the rest of the pack, and hand that particular card over.

D'Abundo produced enlargement of the field of vision by suggestion.

Brémaud ascribed the increased power of vision in hypnosis to an increase of attention. Attention is certainly increased, but that, in my opinion, is not the entire explanation.

The celebrated French philosopher, Bergson, has described one of the most remarkable cases of increased power of vision. This particular case has been cited as a proof of supersensual thought-transference, but Bergson ascribed the result to hyperæsthesia of the eye. In this case a subject who seemed to be reading through the back of a book held and looked at by the operator, was really proved to be reading the image of the page reflected on the latter's cornea. The same subject was able to discriminate with the naked eye details in a microscopic preparation, to see and draw the cells in a microscopical section, which were only 0·06 cm. in diameter. Sauvaire, after some not quite irreproachable experiments, supposed the existence of such a hyperæsthesia of sight, that a hypnotic subject recognized non-transparent playing-cards by the rays of light passing through them. A case of Tagnet's, in which an ordinary piece of cardboard was used as a mirror, is said to have shown quite as strong a hyperæsthesia. All objects which were held so that the reflected rays from the card fell on the subject's eye were clearly recognized.

I have frequently demonstrated visual accentuation in another manner. A subject in the hypnotic state after a time may get fatigued and express a wish for a glass of water. On a table close by there are a dozen empty glasses, all exactly alike. I hand to the subject one of these empty glasses and he drinks from it as if it really contained water. When he puts it down all the glasses are changed in position by some member of the audience, so that no person by the mere look of the glasses could tell which is the one that has been used. After some little time the subject himself may want to drink again, or else it may be suggested to him to have another drink. He will glance over the glasses and to the great astonishment of the audience take up the original one and empty it of its supposed contents.

The subject can be made to *hear with increased acuteness*, and that to an extent apparently marvellous. The ticking of a watch inaudible at more than three feet distance in the waking state becomes audible at thirty-five feet in some hypnotics.

That the *sense of smell* in the hypnotic state may also be made acute is equally easy of proof. A card, paper, envelope, or handkerchief is selected from a number, all alike, and the blindfolded subject is requested to smell it. The object chosen is then put among the rest and the whole packet handed back, when the subject will smell each of them until he gets to the right one, which he gives up, frequently without testing the remainder, so sure is he of his selection.

An experiment in this connection, which I have arranged on several occasions, is the following. The subject is requested to smell a handkerchief, which of course must have no particular smell whatever, and hand it to some member of the audience. To avoid any possibility of mind-reading the operator takes the subject out of the room, while someone hides the handkerchief in some easily accessible place. The subject is led back and told to find the handkerchief. He walks round the room and will soon stop at a place, where he makes a search and discovers the article in question.

I have never tested the increased sense of smell beyond the distance of an ordinary room, but Braid recorded a case in which the scent of a rose was traced through the air at a distance of forty-five feet.

Moll related similar experiments. A visiting-card was torn in pieces, which pieces were professedly found purely by the sense of smell; pieces belonging to another card were rejected. The subject gave gloves, keys, and pieces of money to the persons to whom they belonged, guided only by smell. Hyperæsthesia of smell has often been noted in other cases. Carpenter stated that a hypnotic found the owner of a particular glove among sixty other persons. Sauvaire related another such case, in which a hypnotic, after smelling the hands of eight persons, gave to each his own handkerchief, although every effort was made to lead him astray. Braid and the earlier mesmerists related many such phenomena. Braid, like Moll, described a case in which the subject on each occasion found the owner of some gloves among a number of other people; when his nostrils were stopped the experiment failed. This delicacy of the different organs of sense, particularly of the sense of smell, is well known to be normal in many animals; in dogs, for example, who recognize their masters by scent. Hypnotic experiments teach us that this keenness of scent can be attained by human beings in some circumstances.

An experiment which aroused the keenest interest of neurologists, before whom I have repeated it on several occasions at private séances, is to show that human beings, too, like dogs, can distinguish their fellows by the smell of their clothes. As a matter of fact, they do not really distinguish them in the same manner, but are taught by hypnosis to impute a certain pungent smell to any article of clothing. The subject is brought blindfolded into the room, and smells one person amongst the audience, whom he or she can afterwards recognize by this transferred (really non-existing) smell almost instantaneously.

That the *sense of touch* is accentuated in hypnosis and subsequently in the waking state can be easily demonstrated by giving the blindfolded subject a penny coin to feel, and putting the same amongst a dozen others, he will distinguish the coin chosen from the rest by fingering it.

On the skin two sharp points can be distinguished at less than normal distance, when in the ordinary state they would be taken as one. The sense of touch is so delicate that according to Delboeuf a subject after simply poising on his finger-tips a blank card drawn from a pack of similar ones, can pick it out from the pack again by its "weight."

That the sense of touch is quickened in the subconscious state can be tested also in the following manner. Six objects—I generally choose glasses—are put on a table. The subject looks away or may be blindfolded. Someone selects one of the glasses which I am to touch. The subject is then requested to find the "magnetized" glass, which he does without hesitation.

Frequently I do not even touch the glass, but hold two extended fingers over it. It would appear that in doing this the temperature of the air contained in the glass is slightly raised, sufficiently at least to be recognized by the subject.

I have made movements with a finger at a distance of three to six feet, as if tickling the nose of the subject—who is blindfolded—-and produced sneezing; and similar movements elsewhere to the bare skin excited irritation, and consequent scratching by the subject. If this hypersensibility does exist, we cannot deny it to such persons, as, for example, the *water diviners*. Because a process or event is inexplicable in the light of our present knowledge, this is no reason to deny its possibility.

According to Grasenberger, Sommer, Haenel, and others the rod held in the hands of the diviner of water or of certain minerals deflects downwards by a momentary relaxation in the tension of the muscles, and this is apparently caused by a super-sensitiveness to electric currents in the soil; for the physicists Haschek and Herzfeld, who have made very thorough tests at the Physics Institute of the University of Vienna with a dowser, have come to the conclusion that the dowser is sensitive to differences of electrostatic vibration fields, enabling him to indicate the soil under which there is a stream of water or linear mineral lodes. What most sceptics forget is that the diviner is "human." Even the most perfect machine will fail sometimes.

Both the sense of *temperature* and the sense of *taste* can be tested by pouring water into a number of glasses and holding two fingers over one. The subject will taste each till he gets to the "magnetized" one, which he hands to the operator. Mesmer spoke of mesmerized water, but this idea was scouted and rejected as absurd. But everyone who has studied mesmerism, and tried the experiments, knows that water may be so charged with some force that a person in the mesmeric sleep, without the slightest knowledge that the experiment is made or intended, instantly and infallibly distinguishes such water from that not mesmerized. It is generally described as having a peculiar taste, not easily defined, but different from ordinary water.

Moll says: "That a magnetized person may at times discern 'magnetized' water is correct. It has, however, nothing on earth to do with magnetism. In the first place, it is often impossible to prevent a slight rise in the temperature of water that has just been magnetized. Secondly, it is highly probable that in the act of magnetizing, which is generally accompanied with the gesture of flourishing something in the direction of the water, chemical substances may be introduced into the latter, and may bring about an alteration in its taste. But chemical dissociations have nothing in common with magnetism, which is supposed to represent a physical force. This intentional confusion between chemical agencies and the magnetic force is a good proof of the want of clearness prevailing on the subject amongst most mesmerists."

Why should Moll assume there is a "gesture of flourishing something in the direction of the water" or the still more abominable insinuation that "chemical substances may be introduced" surreptitiously into the water? These are genuine scientific experiments not done for profit but from the mere desire for knowledge, and surely no scientific man is either such a fool as to make flourishes or signs to spoil his own experiments, or such an impostor as wilfully to deceive his audience. Scientific men may differ as to their explanation of such phenomena, but they should not bring accusations against one another without some shade of evidence.

The experiments upon hysterical patients with different *medicines in sealed tubes* performed by Bourru, Burot, and Luys, producing the effects of the drugs they contained—sleepiness in the case of opium, drunkenness in the case of alcohol—are said to be due probably to suggestion. Not having tried the experiment, I can offer no opinion.

Not merely the senses, but *all the mental qualities are highly accentuated in the state of hypnosis*—probably in consequence of an increased sensibility of the brain centres. In some manner, which we are still unable to explain, we can, by touching different regions of the head, standing behind a subject (previously hypnotized, but now awake), and without any "willing" or suggestion, excite expression of different thoughts and emotions and various dispositions.

By touching symmetrical points on the cranium of a subject in deep hypnosis, various manifestations are elicited, both in word and gesture, such as devotion, anger, benevolence, meanness, kleptomania, repentance, conceit, vanity, anxiety, hunger, etc., as well as combinations of these states when two or more centres are touched at the same time.

Such an experiment naturally suggests collusion. To prove that there is no previous arrangement between the operator and subject, the latter should be perfectly ignorant of what is expected, or a new subject should be chosen. The subject who has been operated on before is occasionally too anxious to excel and guesses what he has to say or do. Moreover, it is not at all necessary that the operator should touch the particular centres: he may let any stranger do so. When the expression is not spontaneous the subject should be asked: "What are you thinking of? What do you see? What do you feel?"

I have never produced any effect by mere "willing," or even thinking of the expected manifestation. Frequently, when I have touched another centre than the one I intended, the manifestation would vary accordingly.

I have excited the same centres by applying a feeble galvanic current, and found that if the right side alone will not respond the left will do so, but the best results are produced by stimulating the identical points on both hemispheres of the brain.

It is argued that mere pressure cannot possibly produce such results even on a highly sensitive brain, for the skull is intervening. Quite so, but it must not be forgotten that the skull is not inanimate matter, but a living substance permeated by nerves and blood-vessels. Mere argument will not upset the fact. Let physicians who practise hypnotism experiment as I have done, without preconceived notions as to what is or is not possible. Thus, by touching one particular region of the head, the subject will exhibit a beautiful picture of devotion. Humility is intensely pre-eminent in his gesture. Sometimes he will kneel and pray with a fervour and intensity of expression which it would be difficult to surpass. The moment the finger is removed, he will leave off abruptly, sometimes at a syllable, breaking the word, and when we put the finger down again, he will continue at the same syllable, where he had left off. When another part is touched, he will exhibit pride and hauteur to a most ludicrous degree. In another part, the expression changes to compassion; while in another the most appalling mimicry of fear and misery is produced. Touching another region, the subject can be made to steal, but the moment we shift the finger to the top of the head, the stolen object is returned with expressions of remorse, as if there were a moral region in the brain. The expression of the emotions thus roused is simply wonderful, and I have a collection of photographs reproducing them.

Many of the old mesmerists and hypnotists, such as Gregory, Elliotson, Braid, etc., about whose honesty there can be no question, have obtained the same results; but the experiment is criticized severely by modern investigators who have never attempted to repeat it. There is only one hypnotist, Dr. Pitres, who has made a similar investigation and recorded certain *zones idéogènes*. Braid's acknowledgment should certainly be accepted, since he was not a supporter of that school which believed in a multiplicity of centres in the brain.

Silva, Binet, Féré, and Heidenhain claimed that they could move single limbs of the hypnotized person by stimulating the parts of the head which correspond to the motor centres of the limbs concerned. Challender even proposed to study the physiology of the brain in this way. On the other hand, Boris Sidis, the well-known American psychologist (*Psychology of Suggestion*, 1910), denies the possibility of exciting mental zones. He tells the patient: "Now I am going to touch that part of the cranium which corresponds to the movement of the left arm, and this arm will go into convulsions." He then touches the part, and immediately the left arm is convulsed. I can only repeat that verbal suggestion is stronger than any physical influence.

No one who has ever seen these wonderful manifestations can suppose that the state of the subject is a mere reflection of the operator's mind. For while the latter is tranquil, the former may be heaving with emotion; on the other hand, accidental emotions in the operator are not communicated to the subject, who may be acting some passion or feeling to the life, while the operator is convulsed with laughter, and yet the subject is not thereby affected at all.

I have never seen reason to believe that I have heightened the effect of my processes by exerting the strongest will, or lessened them by thinking intentionally of other things. So far from willing, I have at first had no idea of what would be the effect of my processes.

Again, I would remark, that I have taken all precautions to avoid the possibility of deception.

Firstly, the subject is absolutely unacquainted with what is expected of him, and ignorant of any brain-theory. Yet he will, if a good medium, respond to the touch instantly wherever it may be made.

Secondly, the same results are produced, and have been produced by a stranger, equally ignorant as the subject, being put *en rapport* with him while I was talking to somebody in the room. Yet here also the manifestation has come out as well as before.

Again, it often happens that a wrong result is produced, for example, when an operator knows what to expect and intends to touch a particular part of the head, but turning to speak to someone, touches a wrong centre.

It may be held that this experiment of exciting brain centres to activity taxes the credulity over much. But there is no obligation on anyone to accept my statement. All I wish is to record my observations—made with every precaution possible—in the full belief that future investigators will acknowledge them at some time or other.

CHAPTER VII

EXALTATION OF THE INTELLECTUAL POWERS IN HYPNOSIS

It is acknowledged by practically all observers that the memory for long-past events is much better in hypnosis than in the waking state. Even long forgotten experiences can be revived in that state; in fact, the *exaltation of the memory* is one of the most pronounced of the attendant phenomena. The conscious memory in most persons is weak and untrustworthy; while the subconscious memory, which is accessible only in abnormal and supernormal states, is both extensive and unfailing.

One of the most remarkable effects of hypnotism is this recollection of circumstances and the revival of impressions, the images of which had been completely lost to ordinary memory, and which are not recoverable in the ordinary state of the brain. Nothing is ever forgotten, though we may not be able to recall it. All the sensations we have ever experienced have left behind them traces in the brain so slight as to be intangible and imperceptible under ordinary circumstances; but by influencing the subconscious mind—that storehouse of memories—by hypnotic technique, they can be recalled at the command of the operator.

In hypnosis, as in dreams, the store of memory is unlimited. Sleep cannot be the cause of it, for the hypnotized subject, as already explained, is not asleep. The true cause, it seems to me, can only be the disappearance of the normal habitual consciousness; for in fever and in the dying, as the ordinary consciousness diminishes, there is often a vivid recollection of events long passed. Possibly also the closure of the eyes may be a factor, the sense of sight, the chief inlet of external impressions, being no longer active.

If in hypnosis and its connected states the subject is carried back, of his own or by suggestion, to a remote period of his life, all the forgotten impressions reappear. *Everything learned in normal life can be remembered in hypnosis, even when it has apparently been long forgotten.* Benedikt related a case of an English officer in Africa who was hypnotized by Hansen, and suddenly began to speak a strange language. This turned out to be Welsh, which he had learned when a child, but had forgotten. The subject can be made to recite poetry or whole pages of literature, which perhaps he heard only once or a long time ago. Ricard *Physiologie et Hygiène du Magnétisme*, Paris, 1844) knew a young man with average memory who in hypnosis could recite almost verbally a book that he had read the day before, or a sermon which he had heard. I have repeatedly restored lost memories in hypnosis and made them permanent in the waking state.

I once asked a subject in the somnambulic state to sing something. She replied that she could not sing, for she had never learned to sing. I then asked her whether she could recite, but she said that although she used to recite she had given it up for years, and had forgotten all she had learned. "Try and recollect something," I requested her, but in vain. "Well, tell me a piece you used to know." After some hesitation came the reply, "Tennyson's *Maud*." "Go on, then, recite it!" "Oh, I don't know it." "Yes, you do! You see, you are recollecting it now! It is coming back to you, word for word." And the good lady recited the poem, until I stopped her, although she got no prompting from me, consciously or unconsciously, for I was ignorant of the words.

The *time sense* is evidently extraordinarily stimulated in hypnosis; for nearly all experimenters bear witness to this fact. No matter what time is given, and whether days, hours, minutes, or seconds, at which a post-hypnotic suggestion is to be carried out, the subject will do so faithfully at exactly that period. It appears wonderful to most people that an event should take place at whatever time we may have suggested to the subject while in the concentrated state, whether one, two, or twenty-four hours, or one thousand or two thousand minutes, or in a month, or more remote periods from the day and hour on which a subject has been hypnotized. No deep hypnosis is necessary; light hypnosis is equally successful.

Milne Bramwell (*Hypnotism*, 1906) relates many successful experiments of this kind, for example, the following: A woman was told that in so many thousand minutes she was to write her name, the hour of the day, and the date. She was not well educated, and therefore not likely to work out the number of hours and minutes successfully; and yet, at the time appointed, she wrote down her name and put the date and hour, and was surprised to find what she had done.

In another case, he told a young lady, age nineteen, to make the sign of the cross after the lapse of 4,335 minutes. In spite of the fact that she had forgotten all about the suggestion, she fulfilled it accurately.

The late Professor Delboeuf, of Liège, also made some interesting experiments on the computation of time by somnambules.

There are numerous cases on record in which a subject has been ordered to go to a certain person's house at a certain time and deliver some message. As the time approaches he is seen to be restless till he sets out for his destination. He pays no attention to the people he may meet, and if they purposely delay or hinder him, he forces his way onwards, delivers his message, and can only say that he felt he had to do so.

The sense of time appears to be an innate mental power, for there have been cases of idiot boys who were able to state the time correctly, no matter how suddenly the question was put to them.

It would appear that our subconsciousness is marking time very accurately, without our being aware of it, and at the suggested moment an impulse arises which arouses our consciousness. Even when we are not hypnotized, but suggest to ourselves certain acts to take place at a particular time, the event will so happen at the time indicated. Many people on going to bed, as already mentioned, can "will" to awake at a certain hour.

When the mind is made up to perform a certain action at a given time, the idea is then dismissed from consciousness; but if the subconscious mind has been properly trained, at the definite time, or reasonably near it, the action will be performed, although neither the thought of the time nor the idea of performing the action may have been in the mind from the moment that the resolution was taken. I have often tested myself in this way, to do a certain thing at a particular time, or, what is more wonderful, to remember something which I could not recall at the moment, on the following day at a definite hour—and exactly at the time suggested to myself—the right ideas came to my mind.

Persons with a gift for *music*, latent or only feebly manifested from lack of opportunity or insufficiency of training, can have their natural disposition stimulated to a high degree by post-hypnotic suggestion. For example, a boy with a natural talent for music, but who had practised little, was told by me during hypnosis that he would compose during the day a "sonata" of his own, and play it to me when I called the next afternoon. By permission of his parents I brought a distinguished musician with me, and the boy played his composition to us. The approval of my musical friend was a source of great encouragement to the boy to persevere of his own will without further suggestion by me.

Braid had an experience which attracted considerable attention at the time. One of his subjects, a young work-girl, who did not know the grammar of her own language and who had never been taught music, though she must have possessed the gift, correctly accompanied Jenny Lind, the great singer, in several songs in different languages, and also in a long and difficult chromatic exercise, which was specially improvised to test her. (*Medical Times*, vol. xvi, p. 602.)

Subjects with a talent for *mimicry* can imitate in hypnosis any variety of characters that are suggested to them; and it will be seen that the gestures and voice, the manner and expression, the whole physiognomical and natural language of the emotions are extremely perfect. The attitudes of pride, humility, anger, fear, kindness, pugnacity, devotion, or meditation, and all the others are, with peculiarities in each case, depending on the idiosyncrasy of the individual, profound studies for the artist.

The attitudes and gestures are equal to or surpass the best efforts of the most accomplished actor, although the hypnotized subject may be a person of limited intellectual cultivation, and show no particular talent for mimicry in the normal state. Everyone knows how difficult it is to place oneself in a particular position so that the expression, the attitude, and the actions should correspond to the idea. To represent such a situation as naturally as possible is the greatest art of the actor, but it is still more difficult to change the mood in a moment and pass from one situation to another in a few seconds. The hypnotized subject, however, does so easily.

The hypnotized subject, in impersonating suggested characters, is really not "acting a part" in the ordinary sense of the words. It is much more than acting, for the subject believes himself to be the actual personality suggested, just as the excellence of a real actor is proportionate in each case to his ability to forget his own personality, and to identify himself with that of the character which he seeks to portray. The subject will impersonate to perfection any suggested character with which he is familiar, and his success is accounted for by the fact that his own personality is completely submerged under the influence of suggestion, and he believes himself to be the actual person suggested.

The essential mental conditions of good acting are therefore present in perfection. It follows that in proportion to the subject's knowledge and intelligent appreciation of the salient characteristics of the suggested personality will the rendition approach perfection.

Not only acting, but *dancing* can be perfected in the state of hypnosis. Ordinary people of no education sometimes move in hypnosis with the grace of the most accomplished ballet dancer. Braid attributed the perfection of the art of dancing in the ancient mysteries to this state. I knew and examined some years ago at the Palace Theatre in London Mademoiselle Magdeleine, who had an exquisite skill in the portraying of emotions in hypnosis, and though she had never been taught, executed dramatic scenes and dances which were entirely unknown to her, responding to the musical accompaniment and interpreting its themes to the astonishment of all critics. She exhibited her art all over the Continent as well as in London.

In hypnosis *all latent talents can be stimulated.* Those who are artistically inclined, but unaware of their talent, will want very little training to bring their gift to perfection. I have seen all kinds of art work by persons who had never attempted it before, and I have arranged exhibitions of their products which excited unanimous admiration. The development of innate artistic talents in hypnosis is confirmed by G. de Dubor. (*Mysteries of Hynosis*, 1922.)

In hypnosis the attention is devoted to one train of ideas. There may be such concentration of the nervous energy on one faculty as to render it exalted, no matter whether the hypnosis is self-produced or induced by another. This matter is of great importance, for if the mental powers by the process of hypnosis can be accentuated in their activity and new or unsuspected capacities manifest themselves in that state, it is possible that certain persons can put themselves in that state by a habit of profound abstraction and may be capable of higher things than in the ordinary conscious state. Patients of mine, who have been impressed by their rapid recovery, have asked me whether I can show them how to improve their mental powers. In consequence, many of them have solved problems which they had attempted in vain before, and others have had inspirations for their particular work of the utmost practical utility, such as inventing or improving machinery.

The hypnotic state, as I have shown, is a state of abstraction and exaltation. Of exaltation in the normal state the biographies of all men great in the pursuit of their special subjects or objects bear evidence. Ever with an intense purpose, they follow their particular study, devoting the energies of their bodies, the vigour of their minds, to the soul-pervading idea.

The exaltation is due to the intensity of the prolonged self-concentration on one idea or one series of ideas. Their concentrated devotion to one purpose causes one set of ideas to engross them and to exalt the particular faculty with which they are endowed. To the man with exalted faculties a simple suggestion suffices to excite original power, as when Newton conceived the law of gravitation from the incident of a falling apple.

The brain organ for the particular faculty seems to attract all the nervous energy, while the other centres and corresponding activities remain quiescent. That there is some inherent capacity for increased output of nervous energy in all of us may be shown by a simple example. For instance, I may be able to lift a certain weight; but if I will my arm for some reason to lift a heavier weight, or not to get fatigued by lifting the same weight repeatedly, I can do so. Now, what is the power that gives me the additional strength? It is also well known that under some powerful emotion we possess increased strength and endurance. How is that achieved? Herein lies the value of enthusiasm for one's work, and of high aims and ideals, which can be artificially created by sheer will, special motives, or by suggestion in hypnosis or self-hypnosis. People who work only because they must, or in order to live, can never do as much, either as regards quantity or quality.

When an idea predominates so that all other ideas and activities are nullified, such mental abstraction is notable among many persons of great artistic, constructive, or inventive powers. Such abstraction enables the poet to select and arrange his fleeting thoughts into harmonious symphonies that fill his soul with pleasure, and re-echo through all time in men's hearts. It is the narrowing of their fields of consciousness, the same as in the hypnotized subject, that makes their ideas all-powerful, while others, not connected with the subject of their contemplation, drop out of the field of conscious perception.

Moreover, such abstraction in the right emotional state, accentuated by enthusiasm or ecstasy, renders the vast store of subconscious experiences and knowledge available, and thus makes "inspiration" possible.

The mind of a person in reverie, the same as in the hypnotized person, is so absorbed in a certain train of ideas that it fails to recognize things, persons, or events that are passing about it. Both are oblivious of the hours, and time seems nought to them. In this state of mind, as in hypnosis, there is such a concentration that the external world is obliterated, the body is ignored, and any discomfort that may have pre-existed is now negligible and unnoticed. In the mental ardour of composition, be it literary, pictorial, or musical, the producer is relieved from all bodily woes. Over and over again in the history of men who have created things we find evidence of this glorious ascendancy of mental activity over the distractions of poor surroundings or bodily ill-health. A similar state is that which accompanies the mental concentration of the Indian Mahatmas. It is well known that these men can for long periods ignore even the usually necessary means of bodily subsistence, and it is claimed that in this state of spiritual exaltation powers of insight and of divination become possible to them that to the ordinary man may well seem to approach the miraculous.

That the martyrs of old and the religious ecstatics must have been in a condition of self-hypnosis, and that it is not the power of suggestion or auto-suggestion, but some inherent and still unknown mechanism by which the mind acts on the body, is evident in the light of present-day experience. This has been demonstrated again during the past year by the "wonder" girl, Therese Neumann, of Kornersreuth in Germany, who has been examined by numerous physicians and psychologists as well as official authorities. She is a plain, normal, peasant girl, who ordinarily talks and behaves in quite a natural manner;

but at times she goes into ecstasy, has visions of the crucifixion of Christ, claims to feel the sufferings of Jesus, sheds tears of blood, and bleeds from hands and feet.

Therese Neumann resembles in many respects another devout Catholic and well-known stigmatic—Louise Lateau, of Bois d'Haine, near Mons, who was much talked of sixty years ago. She also could bleed from different parts of the body, which she knew corresponded to the wounds of Christ, by concentrating her attention upon them. The Commission appointed in 1874 by the Royal Academy of Medicine of Belgium to inquire into her case took every possible precaution to detect fraud, and came unanimously to the conclusion that "the stigmata and ecstasies are real" and that "they can be explained physiologically." Indeed, there is no need to ascribe the phenomena of stigmatization either to deception or to a miracle, for we have a sufficient explanation in the process of self-hynopsis induced by intense concentration and spiritual exaltation. Many hypnotists—Charcot, Liébault, Delboeuf, Forel, Jendrassik, and Krafft-Ebing—have produced results of a similar kind in subjects they experimented upon.

The psychical phenomena of religious epidemics have uniformly been induced by the intensified attention being concentrated on one idea, one state of emotion, one form of feeling; other mental and physical faculties being dormant. In religious ecstasy the self-absorption may be aided by fixing the gaze upon some holy figure and, as in the hypnotized subject, the limbs may become motionless, breathing slow, pulse low, and there may be insensibility to temperature, pain, and bodily discomfort. After all, what do we mean by saying that a man "seems hypnotized," but that his whole interest is so concentrated on one point that he neglects everything outside himself and every sensation?

The man in ecstasy over his work is also so concentrated upon some grand idea that he notices no sensations, and locomotion is suspended. He is in a state of disinterested absorption, so far as to forget himself and his earthly needs. This is true, not only of men of genius, but more so of saints and mystics, whose minds are freed from earthly concerns. In ecstasy there is the sleep of the senses and the awakening of the higher faculties; and to the extraordinary concentration must be attributed all those strange acts showing apparent or intermittent anæsthesia and analgesia, which are to be found among men of genius. Marini, when writing his *Adone*, did not feel a serious burn of the foot.

For inspiration, concentration of a passive kind is necessary. The mind must learn to concentrate on the idea of the thing to be realized, without permitting any distraction. And, as in hypnosis, if suitable emotions are aroused, concentration on the desired aim is made easy and the subconscious solution will surge to the surface. The author so concentrated will have his latent ideas from his subconscious store of knowledge penetrate into consciousness. The passion of men of genius for their work enables them to undergo hardship, privation, contumely, and gives them perseverance—that infinite capacity for taking pains which is characteristic of genius. As Schopenhauer said: "genius consists in a pre-eminent capacity for pure contemplation" and "this requires that a man should entirely forget himself." Genius in its own field is most active; while other forms of existence are neglected or temporarily disdained. No energy is left over for other aims and no power remains to be applied in other directions.

In hypnosis there is singleness of aim, so there is in genius. As in hypnosis, so in many men of genius hallucinations are easily induced. Dickens, for example, "amid silence and darkness heard voices and saw objects, of which the revived impressions to him had the vividness of sensations, and the images his mind created in explanation of them had the coercive force of realities. Every word said by his characters was distinctly heard by him." (George Henry Lewes.)

In hypnosis a person is emotionally fired to do what he has not the energy to do in the waking state. The emotional state facilitates attention. The stronger the emotion or passion, the greater the attention. The man of genius is generally a man of powerful emotions, which stir and inspire him. We might just as well attempt to run a steam-engine without fuel or water as to make a genius out of a being without passion.

It is this absorption in things, which the man of genius has set himself to do, and the emotional drive to insistent effort and hard work, by means of which he supplies his subconscious mind with a plenitude of raw material that enables him to have flashes of insight and moments of inspiration.

Like the hypnotized subject, so does genius often find solitude a source of power. No one can create thoughts. The process of thinking consists in holding the mind still and allowing thoughts to arise into it from the depths. If the mind is not kept in the correct state for the matter in hand, it will wander to all kinds of irrelevant matters. Inspiration does not come from effort; on the contrary, it comes often when least expected, and especially when the mind is at ease. Inspiration is nothing more than the sudden awareness of the effects of subconscious thinking, of the silent voice within. It is a process that may be developed by appropriate training.

Inspiration simply fertilizes effort and reduces it to a minimum. Effort, however, cannot dispense with inspiration, and it is in the collaboration of both that the highest and best work is produced. Without rationalized effort and conscious control, even the inspiration of genius is liable to stray. Disordered and uncontrolled inspiration may result in fine work disfigured by lack of proportion, by want of order, by redundance, or other errors.

Subconscious work does not produce weariness like conscious work, that is why men of genius do not tire easily. Bodily energy may give way; but there remains the nervous energy to carry a man over his difficulties and give him the right inspiration.

The inspirations of a man of genius vary according

to his natural gift. He has an intuitive appreciation of some hitherto undiscerned or unexploited significant aspect of life—practical, æsthetic, theoretical, or ethical—to inventive application, philosophical thought, or creative action; and what makes him a genius is the adequate response, with no deviating purpose, to the stimulus constituted thereby. When the moment of inspiration is over, the man of genius becomes an ordinary man. Ovideo justly remarked concerning the contradictions in Tasso's style that "when the inspiration was over, he lost his way in his own creations, and could no longer appreciate their beauty or be conscious of it."

Ecstasy helps inspiration by bringing the subconscious ideas to the surface. The work of genius is nearly all subconscious. Genius divines facts before completely knowing them. For instance, poets create, as Socrates said, not by virtue of inventive science, but just as diviners predict beautiful things, not having consciousness of what they say. As already mentioned, the man of genius often sees the objects which his imagination presents to him. Dickens and Kleist grieved over the fates of their heroes. Painters often visualize the pictures they imagine, reproducing on their canvas what they have thus seen.

Ecstasy is merely a superlative degree of attention. It is a state in which all sensations and thoughts are suspended, except the one which forms the subject of contemplation. The whole mind becomes absorbed in, and concentrated upon, some grand idea. It is a complete detachment of the mind and resembles hypnosis in almost every particular. Indeed, it is brought about by self-hypnosis. As Paul Richter wrote: "The man of genius is in many respects a real somnambulist. In his lucid dream he sees farther than when awake, and reaches the heights of truth."

Many poets have composed their poems in a dream or half-dream. Goethe often said that many of his poems were composed in a state bordering on somnambulism. Klopstock declared that he had received several inspirations for his poems in dreams; so did Seckendorf and La Fontaine. Voltaire conceived one of his books during sleep, and Coleridge, his poem *Kubla Khan.* Tasso, during composition, was like a man possessed. Newton resolved mathematical problems in dreams. Mozart confessed that musical ideas were aroused in him, even apart from his will, like dreams. Hoffman often said to his friends: "When I compose I sit down at the piano, shut my eyes, and play what I hear." Lamartine repeatedly remarked: "It is not I who thinks; my ideas think for me." In Alfieri, Goethe, and Ariosto creation was instantaneous, often being produced just on awakening.

Thus we see that the man of genius manifests many of the phenomena common to hypnosis. His best productions are created in a state resembling self-hypnosis.

CHAPTER VIII

HEIGHTENED SENSIBILITY IN HYPNOSIS. EMANATIONS AND THE HUMAN AURA

Taking a normal subject in the hypnotic state with eyes closed we shall find, without any verbal suggestion whatever, that his sensibility is greatly augmented. Thus passes made with the hand or only one finger above any part of his body, about six inches from it, appear to be felt by the subject, who will move that part in the direction in which the passes are applied. An ordinary horseshoe magnet drawn across in a similar manner will produce a like result.

A magnet held in the operator's hand, in a completely darkened room, will be visible to a hypnotized person, when his eyes are opened, by the luminosity at its poles. The subject can be awakened from his trance and will still see rays of faint light emanating from the magnet.

The hand of the operator has a similar effect on sensitive subjects, faint rays appearing to issue from the tips of the fingers. Absolute darkness is essential, and some subjects require to remain for some time in the darkness before the experiment is commenced. Light from a candle or entering from a chink or cranny may spoil the effect. Of course, one must be careful not to tell the subject what he is expected to see, for that would introduce the element of suggestion.

I have found that ordinary magnetic discs, which are used for hypnotizing people, can be made luminous in the dark by rubbing them between the fingers. The ordinary bronze coin has a similar, though not quite such a strong, effect.

The light which the subject declares to emanate from them is sometimes sufficiently strong to illuminate surrounding objects, which the subject will describe.

The weak point in these observations is that they so largely depend on the good faith of the sensitives, whose testimony is often unreliable, owing to the possibility of hypnotic suggestion causing them to see things subjectively which do not exist in fact, and also because no one in an ordinary state of consciousness has been able to verify the truth of these phenomena at first hand by the use of his senses.

I have seen experiments made in a psychological laboratory to disprove the supposed influence of magnets. A subject was told that a powerful magnet was at work behind his head and tracings were recorded by the proper instruments of his pulse and respiration. Then the subject was told that the magnet had been removed, when actually one was put on, and again tracings were recorded of the pulse and respiration. These tracings were thought to be a proof that the magnet had no power whatsoever, but from what I witnessed I was not convinced, except of one thing, that "suggestion" is stronger than any physical agent. Therefore by telling the patient what is going to happen, the whole experiment becomes worthless. *The subject should never be allowed to know, in the hypnotic state or after, what is expected of him.* When he is told in the hypnotic state, the suggested result takes place immediately; when he is told subsequently in the normal waking state, and we repeat the experiment, the subject is likely to remember the information and he no longer acts automatically or by inspiration, but starts guessing what is required of him, to please the operator or the audience.

In 1845 Karl von Reichenbach, of Vienna, naturalist and technical expert, discoverer of paraffin and creosote, made a series of experiments as to the influence of magnets, etc., on "sensitives," that is people whose powers of perception are exalted above the normal standard by virtue of a highly strung and sensitive nervous system, or those in an abnormal state of consciousness through hypnosis. The results he obtained, although treated with indifference, even contempt, by his scientific contemporaries, are so striking in the light of recent research and knowledge that I feel tempted to refer to them briefly. Reichenbach found that when strong magnets were presented to these subjects they saw flame-like appearances proceeding from the poles and sides of the magnets; the same phenomenon was observed in the case of crystals, and, moreover, they asserted they saw "fiery bundles of light flow from the finger-tips of healthy men" in the same way as from the poles of magnets and crystals.

Charcot, the famous French neurologist and hypnotist, believed in the power of the magnet, and produced similar effects, as did the old mesmerists. Bernheim did not believe in the magnet's power. Binet and Féré (*Animal Magnetism*, 1887) claimed that a magnet can effect a transfer of anæsthesia from one side of the body to the other. Boris Sidis (*Psychology of Suggestion*, 1910) also tried the effects of magnets. He made the verbal suggestion, "I shall change the direction of the magnet, and the transfer will take place from the arm to the leg." Accordingly, "at the end of a minute, the arm fell and the leg was raised."

I have already explained that suggestion is stronger than physical influence. I cannot, however, agree with Tamburini's view that magnetic force has no influence, that "it is only the temperature of the metal which has effect."

Milne Bramwell (*Hypnotism*, 1906) said on this point: "The enigmatic reports of the effect of magnets and metals, even if they be due, as many contend, to unintentional suggestion on the operator's part, certainly involve hyperæsthetic perception, for the operator seeks as well as possible to conceal the moment when the magnet is brought into play, and yet the subject not only finds it out at once in a way difficult to understand, but may develop effects, which (in the first instance, certainly) the operator did not expect to find."

Albert Moll (*Hypnotism*, 1909) mentioned Babinski's and Luys's experiments. "If a hypnotized subject and a sick person are set back to back, a magnet put between them will cause the sick person's symptoms to pass over to the hypnotized subject. Hysterical contractures and numbness have been thus transferred, as also the *symptoms* of organic disease. The transference is said to take place even when the hypnotized subject has no notion what the sick person's symptoms are—i.e. when suggestion is excluded. Luys went even farther. When he placed a magnet first on a sick person's head and then on a hypnotized subject, the morbid symptoms of the first person were supposed to appear in the hypnotized person." Moll's explanation was: "In these experiments of Babinski and Luys we have an obvious combination of the phenomena of mineral and animal magnetism. It is a significant fact that such assumptions as these have hardly ever been made in recent times by men who must be taken seriously. We are, therefore, justified in now assuming that the results obtained by Babinski and Luys in these experiments were due to suggestion—i.e. that there was self-deception on the part of the experimenters, who at the time were not so well acquainted with suggestion as a source of error as we are to-day. Of course, all this does not prove that it is *impossible* for the magnet to influence human beings."

Professor Obersteiner, the celebrated neurologist of Vienna, supposed that there may possibly be a special magnetic sense, which may come into activity with many people during hypnosis, and which is, perhaps, localized in some terminal organs whose functions are still unknown.

Mere passes by the operator's hands have often a soothing effect on persons suffering from pain. I need only remind the reader of the case I have mentioned of a patient suffering from the agonizing pains of a cancerous growth, whom I calmed after all medicinal remedies had failed.

That the operator's hands convey something to objects *touched* by him was shown at the Congress of Experimental Psychology in 1922, when Mr. Henry Sausse showed a similar experiment. He took a card, which someone else had chosen from a new pack, and, *after holding it for a few seconds in his hand,* replaced it in the pack, without having looked at it, The pack was shuffled and given to the subject, who had no knowledge of the identity of the card which had been handled by the experimenter, and yet, on going through the pack, was invariably able to pick out the right one.

A. Bué and Liébault conducted some experiments to prove that a living being can, merely by his presence, exercise a salutary influence on another living being, quite independently of suggestion. And is not that the experience of everyone who has ever felt sorrow or been ill? The child who has just fallen down and is weeping and screaming stops suddenly if his mother softly rubs the bruised spot. Who will deny that when he has been suffering or troubled the soft pressure of a beloved hand upon his forehead has suddenly comforted him? Bué restored the vitality of diseased organs by placing his hands on them or making pressure over them. If the "King's touch" of old had not had a salutary influence, it would not have persisted for so long. How could the thought of healing heal, if the brain, under the influence of this idea, did not constantly send into the diseased organs some currents which restore or regularize their functions?

Albert Moll has pointed out that an influence may be exercised on nerves at a certain, though perhaps very limited, distance; this was admitted also much earlier by Alexander von Humboldt, and his opinion was concurred in by Reil. More than once the hypothesis has been put forward of electrical activities being called up by mesmeric passes, for instance, by

Rostan and J. Wagner. Tarchanoff has demonstrated that the application of gentle stimuli to the skin will excite in it slight electric currents, and that, moreover, a strong effort of concentration of the will, with the muscular contraction by which it is invariably attended, will also suffice to produce the same.

It is not unlikely that the human organism is something akin to a radio-active body, for if our experiments do not deceive us, the body emits rays which can be seen and felt by sensitive persons. That they can be *seen* I have already shown. The following is an experiment, which I have often repeated, which would prove that they can also be *felt*. A person previously hypnotized and now awake and blindfolded is made to distinguish my hand from a dozen others, *when held above his or her hand, at a distance of six inches or less for a few seconds*. This is done with great success, and if we give the different persons numbers, the subject will after a time even recognize when the hand of No. 5 or 7, or any other, comes round again. This experiment would point to different *emanations* from different people and a discriminative sensibility for them in certain subjects in the hypnotic state. Possibly the sensations may be due entirely to hypersensitiveness to the temperature of the different hands, and this is one of the explanations offered by some of the critics; even so, the performance would be remarkable; but I cannot think that there is sufficient difference in the temperatures of the various hands to be perceived even by the most sensitive subject.

Braid observed that hypnotized subjects recognize things at a certain distance from the skin, and this by the increase and decrease of temperature. They walk about the room with bandaged eyes or in absolute darkness without striking against anything, because they recognize objects by the resistance of the air and by the alteration of temperature. Poirault and also Drzewiecki found the same.

Edmund Gurney maintained that there must be a special effluence or emanation to account for the fact that a peculiarly susceptible subject could discriminate the passes made by his magnetizer over an arm or finger, though carefully blindfolded and screened off. The effect produced sometimes amounted to complete local anæsthesia, whilst passes of other hypnotists produced no effect.

Professor Blondlot, of Nancy, announced in 1903 the discovery of certain radiations from the human body, called by him N-rays. Their existence has been denied, although Professor Becquerel showed that animals put under the influence of chloroform cease to emit these rays, but as soon as the influence of the anæsthetic passes off the emission of the radiations recurs.

There is certainly some measurable energy given off by nerves and nerve centres. Professor Charpentier demonstrated that their emission was greatly augmented during functional activity, such as speaking or putting a muscle into action. Even the act of attention and mental effort was found to increase their activity, which was shown by the increased phosphorescence of the platino-cyanide of the barium screen used for that purpose.

J. L. Farny, a Swiss physicist, and K. Müller, Director of the Salus Institute in Zürich, claim that the human body gives off rays, especially on the inside of the hands and at the finger-tips; for they found by experiment that the electric conduction of certain substances which come in contact with these rays is thereby influenced. Apparently these rays, called by them R-rays, arise from the blood stream, for when there is an open wound in the hand the electric conduction of these substances is greatly increased.

These radiations are too faintly luminous for ordinary perception. If, however, we go down the scale of animal life we shall find examples of luminous phenomena apparently of nervous origin. For instance, among the beetles we find two sub-orders which have the power of emitting light—the glow-worm and the fire-fly. Other examples of luminous phenomena in connection with nervous tissues are to be observed in the light which proceeds from the eyes of some animals and insects, especially when seen in the darkness. In the case of some moths, the light emitted is distinctly violet; cats and dogs give out green; whereas the light from the human eye is orange or red. Certain magnetic phenomena are also attended with luminosity, such as the glow in Crookes's tube in the production of X-rays, and the aurora borealis.

Reichenbach claimed to have observed a similar phenomenon in dead bodies and attributed it to chemical action. He claimed that all chemical action is attended with the emission of what he called "odylic" light as well as odylic influence. He held that the chemical changes of decay in dead bodies are sources of such light, just as are the changes in the living body, and he explained thereby how sensitive persons see luminous appearances over churchyard graves in the dark of the night. There will be found in the work of Reichenbach several most interesting and instructive cases of this nature, and thus we find that science, with her touch, dissipates the shades of superstition. Corpse-lights exist, but they are not supernatural; neither are those who habitually see them "uncanny." The lights are perfectly natural and harmless, and the seers are only sensitive persons.

More recently Dr. Paul Joire (*The Annals of Psychical Science*, 1906) has also detected nerve rays, and has measured them. He has proved, moreover, that the nervous energy can be exteriorized in various other bodies. This he demonstrated at the International Congress of Psychiatry in 1907 (see *Lancet*, September 28th) by an instrument of his own invention—the Sthenometer.

The sthenometer consists essentially of a horizontal circular dial, marked out in 360 degrees, in the centre of which, balanced by a pivot on a glass support, is a light needle or pointer, most frequently made of straw. One arm of this pointer is much shorter than the other, and is weighted by a counterpoise to keep it in a horizontal position. The whole is covered with a glass shade. All possible sources of error having been eliminated, such as the action of heat, light, electricity, and sound, by special tests, it was found that when the extended fingers of one's hand are brought near the side of the shade without touching it, at right angles to the pointer, after a few moments, in the majority of cases, a decided movement of the pointer takes place, it being attracted towards the hand. This movement extends over fifteen, twenty, and sometimes up to forty and fifty degrees.

Dr. Joire observed also that not only do the extended fingers produce movements of the sthenometer needle, but also that certain substances which have been held in the hand produce movements, which, previous to being handled, caused no movement, thus proving the exteriorization of this nerve energy. The amount of movement varies with the nature of the substance, some materials giving no results at all. In all cases it was found that the movement was not so powerful as with the hand which previously fingered them. The objects which have been found incapable of storing this force are tinfoil, iron, cotton, and those capable of storing it in different proportions are wood, water, linen, cardboard.

Dr. Henry A. Fotherby recently called attention to the analogy of nerve force to magnetic force. He points out, among other facts, that the energy of sound and light is seen to be capable of conversion into nerve energy through the mechanism of special receiving organs, the ear and eye respectively; just as the energy of sound and light has physically been converted through the mechanism of the telephone and telectroscope into electricity and back again into sound and light.

Féré (*Mémoires de la Société de Biologie*, 1888) was the first to discover the effect of the emotions on the galvanometer. Tarchanoff; Veraguth; C. J. Jung, of Zürich; and F. Peterson, of Columbia University, made further observations and claimed to be able to measure the emotions. They showed that if the body of an individual is introduced into the circuit of a mirror-galvanometer through which a weak current is passing, and the resistance being so arranged by means of a rheostat as to enable them to bring the needle to zero on the scale, psychical conditions will lead to a deflection of the needle of the galvanometer. The inference is that the psychical change produces some physical change by which the current passes less readily or more readily through the body. If the individual is spoken to, or read to, indifferent words have no effect on the galvanometer, but as soon as words are uttered that evoke an emotional tone, an effect is produced on the galvanometer. Every stimulus accompanied by an emotion caused in normal people a deviation in the galvanometer, recorded upon a kymograph as a curve; the amount of such deviation, or height of the curve, being in direct proportion to the liveliness and actuality of the emotion aroused. The stimuli were of the most varied kind—for example, the threat of a needle, of a weight to fall, or its actual fall with a loud noise, arithmetical calculation, sudden call by name, and so on; and the resulting curves were found in normal people to vary directly in amplitude according to their unemotional and phlegmatic or excitable temperament. Successive stimuli delayed and diminished the response.

About thirty-five years ago Professor Savary d'Odiardi in Paris invented an instrument for proving the existence of rays from the eyes and brain.

Professor Ekripsy, of the Electrotechnical Institute,

Leningrad, also invented an apparatus for the measurement of the human rays.

Professor Cazzamali (*Zeitschrift für Parapsychologie*, Leipsic) has invented an apparatus for demonstrating electro-magnetic waves sent out by the brain and affecting sensitive instruments in the room. He describes them as cerebral radio-waves of short length.

Sir Jagadis Chandra Bose, the well-known Indian biologist, demonstrated rays emanating from the human eye, and he, too, constructed an apparatus for their measurement. It is a sort of electroscope sensitive to very fine currents. Concentrating the sight on the instrument by mere will-power moves a needle registering the amount of energy in the ray.

Dr. Charles Russ (*Lancet*, July 30, 1921) is another investigator who invented an instrument which can be set in motion by the mere impact of human vision. He had reflected on the fact that the direct gaze or vision of one person soon becomes intolerable to another person, and this suggested to him that there might be a ray or radiation issuing from the human eye. Dr. Russ has given demonstrations with his apparatus before various scientific societies.

Now let me point out the significance of these investigations.

We know our friends not only by their visible forms and features; we know them also by the magic atmosphere which surrounds them. At least some of us do; perhaps those who are gifted with a special sensibility of that kind. We have also a feeling that a friendly person is in the house or room, though we cannot see him. Again, two perfect strangers meet, and they are drawn to one another before they speak, as if there was an affinity between them; two others meet, and they repel each other.

Even the moods we are in are sometimes conveyed to our friends, without a word being spoken and without any change in the facial expression.

Lavater believed that the eye of a man of genius had emanations; that rays of light, at any rate, reflected from it in a manner peculiar to itself; and that it is thus productive of stronger sensations in the observer than the eyes of ordinary men.

The rays emanating from the eyes and able to move a needle suspended by a slender thread from a delicate instrument, as invented by Russ and Bose, would explain the ancient superstition of certain persons affecting sensitive people with their "evil eye."

The human aura is said to extend from the body for a distance, some say a yard, and gradually fades away. According to Dr. Walter Kilner (*The Human Atmosphere*), who has made the human aura visible to people by scientific demonstrations on a screen, the aura of each person is seen to be coloured according to the vibrations belonging to his prevailing mental state of character. Grey, according to this experimenter, is the fundamental colour of the aura; as intelligence increases, blue becomes the prominent tint, and yellow is the colour of ill-health. The aura is not visible after death.

Each human being generates mental force and sends out thoughts and suggestions not only to the persons of whom he or she is thinking, but in all directions, in the same way as a light projecting its rays from its concentric sphere into space. These suggestions impress other minds which are mentally attuned to them, and have the same vibrations of thought and feeling, just as transmitting and receiving instruments of wireless telegraphy, being attuned, make communication possible; or like two tuning-forks of the same note vibrating sympathetically.

Suggestions reach us night and day from all directions; they are good, bad, and indifferent, joyful or sad, constructive or destructive, and are accepted, rejected, or pass us by, according to the selective action which our subconscious mind possesses. A person who is vibrating at a low destructive rate of fear and worry, will catch similar thought-vibrations thrown out by other people who are in that kind of mood. A person who is vibrating in the joy of life and success, will catch the high vibrations of all the people who are on the same high vibratory level. There are various levels or currents of vibrations of these thought-waves, from the highest to the lowest in mentality and spirituality. We are immersed in them and are affected by them, in the measure as we sympathetically vibrate with them.

CHAPTER IX

SUPERNORMAL PHENOMENA: CLAIRVOYANCE, TELEPATHY, APPARITIONS, PREMONITIONS

AMONG the extraordinary phenomena, which have still to be taken on trust, is one which was familiar to the mesmerists of the past and vouched for by men of learning and good standing, namely *clairvoyance*, that is, the seeing of objects that are invisible to the ordinary sight. Anyone examining the voluminous literature on the subject must admit that at all events some of the experimenters took every possible precaution to prevent self-deception or fraud.

Fraud on the part of the clairvoyant in such test-experiments is not easy. Often there is a double process of blindfolding; since, besides the bandage preventing sight, in cases of deep hypnosis the pupil is usually found to be fixed and insensible to light, as we can test by forcing open the eyelids. In a large proportion of cases also, the pupil is not only fixed and insensible, but is also turned upwards, so that it cannot be seen at all, when the eyelids are forcibly opened. In addition to all this, we can hold the object above or behind the head, positions in which the most sensitive and movable eye cannot possibly see anything.

There have been many honourable men amongst the old mesmerists, men like Herbert Mayo (the eminent physiologist and surgeon of Middlesex Hospital) and John Elliotson (one of the most distinguished physicians of his period, lecturer on Medicine at University College, President of the Royal Medical and Chirurgical Society, the first physician to practise auscultation in England and to use the now familiar stethoscope), who sacrificed their position and income in defence of what they considered a fact and a truth, and these stated positively that many mesmerized subjects do distinguish with their eyes closed the objects placed before them. In the state of somnambulism they have told the number and colour of cards without touching them, and the hour marked on a watch; they have perceived the contents of a closed letter, a sealed packet, or a closed box; they have read several lines of books, opened by mere chance, and distinguished through opaque substances many other things invisible to the ordinary methods of sight.

It has already been pointed out that some "sensitive" hypnotic subjects can see luminous emanations from animals and inanimate objects, as if some radiant force were given out. Considering the latest discoveries in chemistry, should we not look for an explanation in the existence of a peculiar emanation in some forms of matter, the action of which is perceived by certain "sensitive" people, especially when in the hypnotic state?

Perhaps the extraordinary faculty of clairvoyance, which is exercised with perfectly closed and apparently useless eyes, is able to make use of some form of etheric vibrations of a nature analogous to extreme ultra-violet or even X-rays, which can pass straight through solid and opaque substances with little loss by reflection or absorption. If so, is it not possible to conceive of a clairvoyant organ of vision acting independently of the physical eyes and the visual nervous mechanism?

There is a variety of radiations known to us, such as Hertz's electro-magnetic waves, which are employed in wireless telegraphy, and are capable of being used for communication over thousands of miles of space; there are also the rays which are given out by various substances, but particularly by nerves and nerve centres. Then we have heat, luminiferous, ultra-violet, Becquerel, and lastly Röntgen or X-rays, which penetrate solid objects.

May it not be that our modern methods are at fault? It is well known that the early mesmerists constantly and habitually developed higher powers in their subjects. Their experiments were often made, under test conditions, by the most careful and conscientious scientists, and the results are recorded in the many volumes on the subject written at the time.

When did the higher phenomena show the first signs of decadence? A moment's reflection will fix it at about the date of the promulgation of the theory of "suggestion" by Bernheim of Nancy (1886). As soon as it was found that the hypnotic sleep could be induced by suggestion, all other methods were practically abandoned. It was a much easier operation than to make passes over a subject for an indefinite length of time, accompanying the passes by fixity of gaze and intense concentration of mind. The law of suggestion is undoubtedly of the highest significance, but let us remember that it is not the whole of psychic science. It seems clear, then, that it is to this change of methods that we must look for an explanation of the change in results.

In the subject put to sleep by the mesmeric method, by passes without contact, and with no verbal suggestion of any kind, and who has never been hypnotized by any other process (for the memory of past hypnosis by the subject is a great factor in determining the condition of the present state), we have an individual with a personality of his own. Here we must agree with the mesmerists. Instead of an uninteresting automaton, we have a subject whose mental faculties have become clearer and more powerful, and who often exhibits an intelligence and capacities far in advance of his normal condition. This, in their opinion, is the individual who will most readily develop into the clairvoyant, so long as we refrain from making suggestions to him.

Some clairvoyant subjects are able to perceive objects in an adjoining room, in one overhead, or in one below. This used to be a frequent phenomenon, without any special preparation, and was usually brought to light by the subject, of his own accord, remarking what took place there. The experiments I have performed in this respect have not been satisfactory. Thus in one case I asked a subject whether she could tell me what her husband, who was at home a hundred miles away, was doing at that time, then about ten in the morning. She replied that she saw him in the garden with the children. On inquiry I ascertained that the vision, if such it was, was quite correct, but that her husband was in the habit at that time of the morning of taking the children round the garden. There have always been possibilities of ordinary explanation, so that I can offer no evidence of my own. Possibly I should have succeeded with more patience and perseverance, for many of these supernormal manifestations require a good many trials.

Some clairvoyants possess such an extraordinary power, if we may accept the testimony of the old mesmerists and some men of to-day, that they are often able to feel and describe every pain or ache felt by a patient with whom they are put *en rapport*, and will even in some cases feel, or intuitively perceive, the morbid state of certain parts. They will diagnose that the patient has a headache, or a pain in the side, or difficulty in breathing; and will declare that the brain, or lungs, or liver, or stomach, or heart, etc., is deranged in such and such a manner. They seem to have an intuitive perception of health and disease. These subjects seem to be able to give information of the form and situation of various organs, and to describe them with very great precision, though not with anatomical correctness, if the somnambulist be ignorant of anatomy. The human body seems to them as if transparent, and there have been medical practitioners who have availed themselves of this faculty of locality to discover the nature of obscure diseases, using the subject, so to say, as a living stethoscope to assist their own judgment.

Clairvoyance and some of the other phenomena we are about to describe are so unlike any which have been brought within the sphere of recognized science as to subject the mind to two opposite dangers. Wild hypotheses as to how they happen are confronted with equally wild assertions that they cannot happen at all. Of the two, the assumption of an *a priori* impossibility is, perhaps, in the present state of our knowledge of Nature, the more to be deprecated, though it cannot be considered in any way surprising.

In the physical science, it is easy to demonstrate discoveries and to have them repeated under exactly the same conditions. When we come to the science of mind, however, all the circumstances are changed. True, we have our anatomists and physiologists working with the scalpel and microscope, but even as regards the most elementary mental phenomenon, say, man's reasoning capacity, how much have we learned from them? No one will deny that man does reason, and that to animal intelligence human reason must seem something supernatural.

Is it a wonder, then, that to ordinary men the abnormal capacities of the hypnotized sensitive persons should seem incredible? Why should man in the progress of his evolution not have developed powers, and may we say brain functions, of which we have still only meagre knowledge? I do not know if a "clairvoyant" power really exists, but I differ from those who think it impossible. Some of these sceptics have never tried to find out; others have tried but failed. But would they deny man's reasoning capacity because some men arrive at wrong conclusions? Let us not forget man's reasoning capacity has been trained for thousands of years, and we have received systematic schooling in its use throughout our childhood. If there be such a power as "clairvoyance" it must be admitted that humanity has done nothing to draw it out, and that those in whom we discover it lack the training which is necessary for all the mental powers with which man is endowed. Therefore, let us assume a different attitude towards such abnormal phenomena as we cannot explain at present, and while we have given up the explanation of their being supernatural, let us give up the idea that even spontaneous manifestations (and not only their habitual practice for personal gain) belong to deception, fraud, and imposition, and that only highly credulous persons believe them.

Many persons who are extremely averse from admitting the existence of clairvoyance at all are apt to suppose that they can avoid doing so, when the facts are forced on their attention, so that they can no longer be denied, by ascribing them to thought-reading; as if thought-reading, the power of seeing into another man's mind (and through his body too), were at all less wonderful than the power of seeing through a stone wall or a floor.

To my apprehension, thought-reading is still more wonderful and incomprehensible than that kind of clairvoyance which takes note of material things at a distance. In the latter case, we can imagine some subtle, rare medium, by which the impressions may be conveyed to us, as light or sound is. But how do we perceive thoughts, not yet expressed, in the mind of another? It would appear, then, as William Gregory (1847) has said, that those who would explain all clairvoyance by thought-reading, only fall from the frying-pan into the fire. They account for an apparently unaccountable phenomenon by one still more incomprehensible.

The question whether it is possible for one mind to act on another where the two minds do not communicate by the spoken word, or by signs or symbols of any visible kind, has set a great many people thinking, and caused not a few to make observations of their own and to investigate the experiences of others. As a result, those who have studied the subject have no longer any doubt that communication is possible between mind and mind otherwise than through the known channels of the senses, but that such communication is rare, because its manifestations require exceptional conditions. Primarily there must be a mind willing strongly to impress a thought, and the mind of another in that state of subjectiveness or passivity which makes it possible to receive the impression.

An experiment that is frequently performed is that of thought-transmission *without contact*. A number of people, seated in a circle, are requested to think of a particular number or article. The subject, who has been previously blindfolded outside the room, is brought in and led to a seat in the centre of the circle by someone unacquainted with the arranged idea. Certain individuals are so gifted that after a few minutes they will have a vision of the number, or the article, on which the minds of those present are concentrated.

However, it is not with such voluntary and arranged thought-transmission by one or more persons concentrating intently on a word that we are here concerned, but with involuntary transference arising more or less spontaneously and having a definite significance.

Such thought-communication between individuals, especially between close relations and persons in sympathy with each other, is indeed not uncommon, but to produce such a phenomenon *at will* is an activity of a kind different from its accidental occurrence.

We have no notion at present of the process employed in the ordinary communication of subjective minds. *The messages that telepathy conveys appear, as a rule, to be not definite thoughts but feelings or impressions which in some cases raise ideas and in others do not.*

The degree of clearness of the mental image is largely determined by the intensity of its projection and may be intentional or not. The state of clearness and the measure of activity of the operative functions of the mind that receives the message will also affect the result. This clearness will chiefly be determined by the degree of quietude of the mind which obtains at the time. The impression made upon the recipient brain is transferred outwards. In other words, *there is a hallucination produced*, and that hallucination will vary according to the general experiences and knowledge of the recipient. That is why the same message or impression reaching a number of persons may produce a different hallucination in each, and be interpreted accordingly.

If we assume that a nerve-force or some still unknown energy can radiate from the brain (as described in the previous chapter), and that such force may travel and strike another brain, which is in tune with it and is also in a passive state, we have perhaps begun to solve the problem.

That an impression striking a passive brain does produce an image which is transferred outward is not uncommon, and is often caused by other stimuli—electrical, chemical, and mechanical—is evidenced in experiments upon animals. Further, various forms of auto-intoxication may supply the stimulus in certain diseases, as, for instance, in migraine, epilepsy, and hysteria, in which subjective visual phenomena are of frequent occurrence, ranging from flashes of light, plays of colours, to actual hallucinations. The same may also be produced by the alkaloids present in certain poisonous drugs introduced into the system, such as opium, etc. Again, it may be due to some subtle stimulus from one part of the brain acting on another during certain states of consciousness, as in dreams. Why not, then, from one brain to another?

If it be granted that whenever any activity of the brain takes place a chemical change of its substance takes place also, or, in other words, an atomic movement occurs—and let it be granted that no brain action can take place without creating a wave of undulation in the all-pervading ether—why might not such undulation, when meeting with or falling upon duly sensitive substances, produce impressions? And such impressions are "felt," not thought of.

Such oblique methods of communicating between brain and brain would probably but rarely take effect. The influence would be too faint and subtle to tell upon any brain already preoccupied by activities of its own, or upon any but brains of extreme, perhaps morbid, susceptibility. But if, indeed, there be radiating from living brains any such streams of vibratory movements, these may well have an effect even without speech, and be, perhaps, the *modus operandi* of "the little flash, the mystic hint" of the poet—of that dark and strange sphere of half-experiences which the world has neven been without. It is quite permissible to surmise some sort of analogy to the familiar phenomena of the transmission and reception of vibratory energy.

Supposing, then, that all thought is connected with cellular vibrations, we can comprehend by analogy what happens in mental suggestion at a distance. The communicating cerebral zones may be compared with two pianos or two harps which vibrate in unison, or to two tuning-forks which give the same note, and of which the one repeats spontaneously the vibrations given by the other. They may be also compared, as Richet has compared them, with two wireless telegraph stations more or less perfectly attuned. If we suppose two men in whom the cerebral cells vibrate harmoniously, whether in consequence of a bond of kinship or friendship, or because one of them has imposed his rhythm on the other, the thought which causes vibration of the one may be able to make the other vibrate without impressing the various brains which are on the line of the vibrating wave. The brain of the subject impressed plays the rôle of the resonator. The impression produced will arrive much more easily at the consciousness of the subject as the latter is less disturbed by other impressions. That is why it is important to choose for experiments of this character a time when we believe the subject to be disengaged and quiescent.

Purely experimental proof there is none and such will be difficult to obtain. The recent attempts to get owners of wireless receiving instruments to think of certain words which had been put down in writing at the Central Broadcasting Station was no proper test, for in proper telepathy it is ideas and feelings that are conveyed of a certain incident, weighted with emotion, not exact words. And as regards actual telepathy, most of the evidence consists of sporadic manifestations, which may be accepted or denied, according to the trustworthiness of the witnesses and the scepticism or faith of the investigator. In many cases of telepathy, such a long interval has often elapsed between their occurrence and recital that the imagination has had the leisure to fill up the gaps of memory. Others are second-hand or third-hand recitals. Still, there remains a sufficiently large number of authentic cases worthy of credence to allow us to keep an open mind on the problem.

Thought-transference in the days of mesmeric séances was a common phenomenon; whereas hypnotists, practising by the method of suggestion, that is to say, looking on more or less indifferently while the subject hypnotizes "himself," nowadays can obtain no such results. The old mesmerists used to concentrate their attention and exercise all their will power to magnetize their subject. By their passes, fixed gazing, and mental concentration, they almost, if not entirely, hypnotized themselves by the same act by which they mesmerized their subjects. This absorption of the mesmerizers put their subconscious mind into activity, and so it was possible, without a word being spoken, for the mesmerized subjects to receive the impression of the thoughts of the operators.

The brain, from which the thought is sent out or liberated—whether voluntarily or subconsciously—must act, as I have said, with intense force, such as we can imagine is the case when a strong and healthy man suffers death by violence on the battlefield. His entire life-force is sent vibrating through the air, and his thoughts are concentrated with all the power possible upon his sorrowing wife or his child, whom he may never see again, or his father or mother who is anxiously waiting for news from him. On the other hand, the clearness of the impression will depend on the state and degree of quietude of the person receiving it. If the recipient is actively engaged in some occupation, so that his or her own brain is "energizing," no impression can be made.

The passive condition is essential for the successful transmission of telepathic communications. The more perfectly that condition is attained, the better will be the impression. Hence most messages are received in repose or light sleep, or on just going off to sleep, or while resting in a chair in that relaxed state that is very much akin and often leads to sleep. That is why visions occur most often at night. The brain is then resting, or at least not consciously functioning. During the day we are too busy, or rather our brains are too busy, besides receiving a multitude of subconscious impressions from our active and noisy surroundings, so that a subtle impression coming from a distance is likely to pass unnoticed.

The impression may be so slight that it is merely "felt" by the person and its effect is merely that of "uneasiness." It need not raise any ideas at the moment. Or the impression may be so intense that a vision of the sender and the scene during which the message was sent may be projected from the brain and appear as real. A mother experiences a sudden anguish and sees her husband or child in peril in clearly defined conditions. She is able to bear witness that this presentiment or vision occurred exactly at the time when the person being in peril or in danger of death thought strongly of her and transmitted to her by unconscious mental suggestion the image, or the picture of the perilous circumstances in which he was placed. The vision need not be at all accurate. Friends see, as a rule, the person in the clothes that they are familiar with, owing to his having worn them in their company, or they see him dressed in some more or less undefined garment. The reason for this is that it is some form of brain-energy which strikes the passive recipient, who then interprets the message in accordance with his own recollections. It is the person's spiritual image which is transmitted, and not the image of his clothes, or of his beard—which he may have allowed to grow since they saw him last—or of anything material whatever; only his spiritual image, and possibly an image of the form of danger that threatens him and causes his life energy to vibrate. In all cases, the interpretation of the sensation felt, or of the vision seen, will be in accordance with the experiences and knowledge of the recipient.

Such messages and visions are rare because we are so rarely in a "receptive" state. The noises of civilization, not ceasing even at night; the fatigue caused by the strenuous work of the day blunting the sensibility of the nerve-cells and causing sleep to be either too deep or disturbed by dreams; the attitude of indifference of most people to matters spiritual—all these are factors that make it difficult, if not impossible, for such communications to reach our brain or to make an impression upon it. However, we are so accustomed to see things that are not objective realities, and to hear sounds and even voices that have no foundation—in our healthy, active, waking state, as well as in our dreams—that we dismiss them instantaneously as an error of our senses, whenever they occur, and think no more about them. A telepathic communication has therefore very little chance of being accepted. Some people, again, suffer such fear and anxiety regarding the welfare of those whom they love and know to be exposed to injury that they dismiss the impression as the result of their fancy, and frequently it is proved that their fears were quite groundless. Many people will, of course, say: "What a good thing these ethereal communications are rare, for who wants to be disturbed by uncanny visions?" I agree, but this objection is beside the question, which is not whether such experiences are desirable, but whether they are possible.

Assuming life and mind to be forms of energy, the forces sent out by a dying person will be all the greater the younger he is, and the more violent and unexpected the death. There must be a bond of union and sympathy between the sender and the recipient, that is to say, they must be tuned alike to cause the brain cells of the recipient to vibrate alike and produce the vision, or feeling, that something extraordinary has happened.

The emotions attending a death by violence are necessarily of the most intense character. The desire to acquaint the world with the circumstances attending the tragedy is overwhelming. The message is not for a single individual, but to all whom it may concern. A ghost does not travel from place to place and show itself promiscuously, but confines its operations to the locality, and especially to the room in which the death-scene occurred. In the castles of bygone times the walls were thicker, there were fewer and smaller windows, and hardly any ventilation, hence the energy that was created by such a circumstance would cling to the room. Moreover, the room in which a murder occurred would most likely be shut up and never be used again. If, years after, some new tenant inhabits the death-chamber, he may, when in a passive state, receive an impression, which he translates into a vision of the ghost. Then it becomes known that the room is "haunted." One man, pluckier than the rest, says he will sleep in that room and slay the ghost, should he meet him. He waits and waits, sword in hand, but no ghost appears. Then he tires, and just as he is on the point of falling asleep, his brain, too, receives an impression—and the ghost stands before him, frightening him out of his wits, like the rest. This is an explanation which has the merit of reasonableness, and I know of no better to account for the occurrences which are authenticated. This theory, formulated by T. J. Hudson (*The Law of Psychic Phenomena*, 1894), would also explain another peculiarity of ghosts—that they invariably disappear, never to return, when the building which was the scene of their visitation has been destroyed. Another building may be erected on the same spot, but the ghost never reappears. The powerful emanations at the time of danger may account for the fact that the ghosts which are best authenticated, and which seem to possess the greatest longevity, so to speak, are of those who have died under circumstances of great mental stress or emotion. Another salient characteristic, which seems to be universal, and which possesses the utmost interest and importance in determining the true source of the phantasm, is that it possesses no general intelligence. That is to say, a ghost was never known to have more than one idea or purpose. That one idea or purpose it will follow with the greatest pertinacity, but it utterly ignores everything else. A ghost (according to Hudson) is, therefore, nothing more or less than an intensified telepathic vision; its objectivity, power, persistence, and permanence being in exact proportion to the intensity of the emotion and desire which called it into being.

Another form of spontaneous telepathy has relation to some event in the immediate future—in the form of presentiments, premonitions, and premonitory visions.

Quite a number of people have the gift of "pre-vision." For example, they may be thinking of a friend, perhaps one whom they have not seen for years, or one who is most unlikely to pass the locality at the time, and meet him soon afterwards coming round a corner or out of a house; in short, under conditions which preclude the possibility of having seen him earlier, even subconsciously. Of course, these previsions may often be mere coincidences, but the frequency with which they are experienced by certain people suggests a deeper reason for them.

History abounds in instances of psychically sensitive individuals who have manifested upon various occasions a peculiar knowledge, not only of present, although distant occurrences—present in time, but distant in space—but also a presentiment of future events, which have been subsequently verified, to the astonishment of their friends, and of all those who happened to be cognizant of the circumstances. This fact cannot reasonably be denied, whatever difficulty may exist in attempting to account for it.

Possessing some gift in this direction, I have analysed my own sensations in such cases and found that I experienced first of all a "feeling" that I might meet a certain person, or a sensation that I actually see him, but so far away that my eyes could not possibly have seen; then I have reasoned that I was most unlikely to meet that person, and then finally he has stood before me. We have here again something analogous to what takes place in the detectors of the Hertzian waves in the Marconi system of telegraphy. When the known person comes within a certain radius his approach is in a certain way felt, but he is not identified, because this method of feeling is outside the habitual action of our senses, and therefore passes unperceived, our attention not being yet adapted to receive it.

That these previsions, presentiments, and fore bodings often prove wrong is no evidence against the existence of such a psychic faculty, which may consist merely in an extraordinary capacity of noticing significant details that escape other people's observation, together with a power of quickly associating ideas.

There are other wonderful phenomena connected with the state of hypnosis and self-hypnosis, as, for example, automatic writing. I have not dealt with them in this book, for my knowledge of these subjects is only second-hand. I have never produced them.

CHAPTER X

THE OBJECTIONS TO HYPNOTIC TREATMENT

Many people have a wrong conception of hypnotic treatment. What they have in their minds is what they have gathered of hypnosis from the public performances by showmen hypnotists; performances which aim at making the subjects appear ridiculous, in order to excite merriment among the onlookers; the subjects being mostly men who make a living by hiring themselves out for the purpose. Whatever the practice of hypnotism was in former days, the method adopted by qualified medical men to-day varies little from that described in this book, and must be admitted to have nothing objectionable in it.

Very few people have any knowledge of the clinical work done by medical hypnotists. Consequently it is not surprising that they have the false notion that those who practise hypnotism do not take into consideration the causes or deeper sources of the trouble they are treating. They regard hypnotic suggestion as an arbitrary, forceful interference with mental processes; whereas the truth is that hypnosis enables us better to investigate the psychic roots of a neurosis, to lay them bare, and to show the patient what is really troubling him. In hypnosis we can get the patient to recognize frankly those conflicts which he had up till then pushed aside from the sphere of his consciousness and can train him to attempt a proper adaptation to the circumstances in which he lives. Hypnosis is only a state of preparation to penetrate the subject's subconsciousness in order to unravel any complexes which hinder his normal mental life. We introduce nothing which he himself would not desire in his best moments.

Some people assert that in hypnotism the individual is deprived of his own will-power. This is absurd, for *it is the aim of the operator to direct the will-power of the subject, which has become attached to wrong beliefs and wrong notions into normal, healthy channels*. There is some good in everybody, and we create a desire for it so strong that it overcomes the urge towards the unhealthy and evil. The patient does not surrender his will, but exercises it in co-operation with the physician. Of what use, for instance, is the unaided will to the confirmed drunkard? He has no will except to drink. We do not interfere with the normal will of a patient, any more than the physician or surgeon proposes to interfere with normal physical conditions.

Hypnotic treatment, to be successful, must take account of the personality, and there is no more dominance in it than there is in any other form of psychotherapy. The patient is only as much dependent on the doctor as any other man who is ill. Any physician who inspires confidence and belief will make the patient more or less dependent upon him, but it is the business of the hypnotist to teach his subject self-control. Individuality is not destroyed or weakened, but often greatly strengthened by the treatment.

Another objection to hypnotism, also based on the popular belief that the hypnotized subject is deprived of his will, is that he will always tell the truth, so that all his secrets can be obtained from him for the asking. It is upon this assumption that the hypothetical value of his testimony in criminal jurisprudence depends. It is true that, as regards ordinary questions, the truth is always uppermost in the subconscious mind. A subject will often say in hypnosis that which he would not say or remember in his ordinary waking state; nevertheless he never betrays a vital secret.

It has always been said that a hypnotized subject might be made to do foolish things. Certainly he might, if deeply hypnotized, but a physician would gain nothing by making suggestions to a patient which would arouse indignation and disgust in the waking state. The question here is not what mountebanks might do, but what a physician of recognized character and standing can be relied upon to do. If we trust the physician to aid us by drugs or surgery, we can trust him with the hypnotic power. Surely, in the administration of anæsthetics, the loss of will-power is more complete than under hypnosis?

Others betray still more their lack of practical acquaintance with hypnotic treatment by objecting that a subject might follow the suggestions of an immoral or criminal hypnotist. Again, I must repeat that the operator does not impress his will upon the subject. He can only evoke powers which are there already, dormant or conscious. The subject will tend to morality or immorality according to his inborn dispositions and organized habits, whether he be awake or hypnotized. *Criminal suggestions would be accepted only by criminal minds.* Still, I differ from those hypnotists who say, probably in order to allay public fear, that criminal acts cannot be suggested or executed. It can be done in *deep* hypnosis, if the operator is a scoundrel and the criminal deed is presented as a purely innocent act. I cannot understand authorities on hypnotism declaring, on the one hand, what a wonderful power hypnotism is, and on the other that hypnotized subjects can protect themselves against deception by a mountebank or rogue. Nor can I understand those men who, acknowledging its dangers, rail against its practice by properly qualified physicians, who rarely induce the deep stage, and in any case, for their own protection, at all events with female patients, demand the presence of a third person during treatment.

Some people believe that repeated induction of the hypnotic state might endanger the health of the subject. This is certainly not true of the patients who come to consult the physician; for they come to be cured, and in most cases are cured. It is said that hysteria and hystero-epileptic fits not infrequently follow the use of hypnotism; but, in the experience of a lifetime, I have never witnessed any such results. I have read of such complications amongst Mesmer's and Charcot's cases; but both these operators used subjects who were already suffering from hysteria. Instead of supposing hypnosis to be a cause of hysterical attacks, we are far more justified in assuming that when once a complete hypnosis has been obtained we have in our hands a trustworthy means of curing the disorder.

It has been said that hypnotism improperly directed might develop insanity. I have never come across such a case, never heard or read of one. No doubt it is theoretically possible, but only when hypnotism is employed by the ignorant, and what remedy improperly used is not productive of evil? Those who raise such an objection confuse hypnotism with spiritualism and other occult practices. That the constant seeing of supposed apparitions may unhinge the mind of certain people predisposed to insanity is perfectly true, but this fact has nothing to do with the practice of hypnotism.

While some people think hysteria and insanity may develop in hypnotized subjects, others quite mistakenly hold that only hysterical and weak-minded persons can be brought under its influence. Still others believe that only a small number can be hypnotized. What they have in mind is deep hypnosis, which, as I have often repeated, is quite unnecessary for therapeutic purpose.

Then there are a large number of people who do

not deny the good that hypnotism does, but protest, on ethical grounds, against this method of rendering a person healthy and moral. These, too, forget that in modern hypnotism the person is not sent to sleep, and that *we give him that control over his bodily functions and mental dispositions which he himself desires but has not the strength to exercise*. If to relieve pain and suffering, to give sleep to the weary and heavy laden, to give the right ideas and sentiments to the vicious, thus enabling them to become virtuous, if all these, when done in hypnosis, are opposed to ethics, then we ought also to abolish opium, belladonna, strychnine, and other poisonous drugs from the pharmacopœia. The hypnotist is using educational methods just as the ordinary person does, only under more favourable conditions and after persuasive methods have failed. He does nothing which would not be approved of by the normal consciousness and judgment of the subject.

Another common objection is that, after hypnotic treatment, there is a great tendency to relapse. This is certainly untrue. Relapses are not more frequent in hypnotic than in other forms of treatment. On the other hand, no other treatment can show so many rapid and lasting cures. I refer to the cases quoted which are all properly authenticated. This does not say that no relapses ever occur, and here I will explain some of the causes of recurrence of the trouble.

Often we obtain only a one-sided history. We get to know the patient, but not always his or her family.

Where there is a kink in the son or daughter, there may be one also in the parent. The home life is apt to bring out again the defect that has been treated, unless special precautions have been taken. Sometimes there is an unreasonable, domineering father, or a narrow-minded, hysterical mother, who makes life for the patient a misery. Or take the reformed drunkard or a mental patient who has to return to a miserable home and a nagging wife. In other cases the occupation of the patient is such as to bring on fresh symptoms; yet he may not be able to change it. In other words, there may be circumstances over which neither the patient nor the hypnotist has control.

Furthermore, there are diseases which are of a recurrent nature; other diseases remain inactive so long as the patient leads a quiet, uneventful life, of which he sometimes tires; and, finally, there are persons who are constitutionally so defective that no treatment of whatever kind can promise more than temporary results.

Relapses may occur when the ideas presented to the patient were not adapted to his individuality, as may happen when there is no time to study him, as when he comes only once or twice. Or again, when the operator, as is the case in unqualified practice, has neglected to treat the physical condition and has taken no notice of the state of the nervous system which gave rise to the particular disorder, or when the underlying pathological focus has not been reached and dealt with, and the teaching of mental discipline and the re-education of the character of the patient have been omitted.

Any psychotherapist, whether he practises hypnotism, psychoanalysis, or other form of mental treatment, if he has no training and experience in nervous disorders and psychiatry, and in normal and abnormal psychology, may fail to distinguish, for example, the depression of the neurasthenic from the depression of the melancholic, the obsession of the psychasthenic from the fixed ideas of the paranoiac, the lameness of the hysteric from that of the malingerer and from organic lameness, the indigestion of the hypochondriac from nervous dyspepsia and the various organic disturbances of the digestive tract. If the qualified medical man is discouraged from practising a special form of psychotherapy, the inevitable consequence will be that the patients will be driven to the advertising quack with no medical training whatever. The one thing that the patient wants is to get well. He judges by results. He prefers a doctor, if a doctor can help him; but he will not hesitate to go to an unqualified man when orthodox remedies have failed to benefit him.

Of late years psychoanalytic treatment has aroused popular attention. It originated in the hypnotic practices of Drs. Freud and Breuer, and the introductory proceeding is very similar. The patient lies on a couch and the physician, who sits behind him, asks him "to put himself in a condition of calm self-observation, without trying to think of anything, and then narrate whatever comes into his mind." Such a state of reverie resembles very much that of light hypnosis. But psychoanalysis is limited in its application to neuroses and psychoneuroses of a psychical origin, whereas hypnosis may be applied to all functional diseases, and it relieves the symptoms even of organic ones. Moreover, psychoanalytic treatment requires the attendance of the patient day after day for months, whereas the hypnotist is expected to show, and generally does achieve, quick results. If he fails, there is an end of the case.

The true psychotherapist is the eclectic, who uses whatever method will benefit the individual and takes whatever is good and applicable from every form of psychic healing. On the other hand, the Freudian psychoanalyst believes in no other process than his own. The true psychotherapist analyses the whole mind and character of the patient, all his dispositions, hereditary and acquired, normal or abnormal, and searches for the cause of the trouble in the whole instinctive and emotional life of the individual; but the Freudian psychoanalyst traces every neurosis and psychoneurosis to the activities of one instinct alone—the sex instinct.

In psychoanalysis a transference of affection takes place to the person of the physician; not so in hypnosis. In fact, many psychoanalysts declare that without such transference there can be no cure. This transference of emotion to the analyst, together with, and as a consequence of, the deleterious effects of continual and prolonged dwelling upon the real or imaginary love affairs of a person's life, his experiences and his longings, which takes place in psychoanalysis, constitutes a serious objection to this method of therapy. I have never found in hypnosis such a transference to take place. Even if it were possible, the treatment is far too short for such intimacy to arise. Of course, we have all our likes and dislikes of people, and so of the physician. It does happen that women sometimes fall in love with their doctor, hypnotist, or not; sometimes they marry him.

As regards other objections, they are best answered *in toto* by a summary statement of the claims made for hypnotism in this book.

The hypnotic state is a condition of objective passiveness and abstraction with relaxation. Though nearly everyone can be brought under hypnotic influence, there are persons who are better adapted for the process than others, and some who are very susceptible to such influence. Remarkable cures are sometimes achieved by hypnosis with patients who are hardly made drowsy. The hypnotic state is induced not because it is in itself curative, but because that condition is peculiarly favourable to the reception and retention of ideas. Ideas presented to the mind of the patient, which in his ordinary condition would remain unheeded, are in the hypnotic state received with eagerness. With all this there is an emotional tone of exaltation which takes the place of the sense of failure previously present. The altered emotional tone gives new energy. The mechanism of spontaneous healing is the calming of disturbing emotions, which hinder the normal working of the nervous system, and the stimulation of elevating emotions which in turn stimulate the whole organization.

In hypnosis it is particularly easy to bring out of the subconscious mind into active consciousness memories and ideas which have been repressed or upon which the individual has lost his grip by reason of their having become dissociated by fatigue, by friction with the environment, or by other disintegrating factors. By the process of hypnotism we can rectify unhealthy states of mind which tend to misadapt a person to his environment, such as depressing emotions, apprehensions, fear of disease, or of the consequences of social acts, fixed irrational beliefs, illogical doubts and scruples, constant introspection, abnormal self-consciousness, and excessive concentration of the attention on the physiological functions of the body.

The hypnotist does not impress his personality upon the patient, but works in co-operation with him. The very method of hypnosis teaches the subject mental discipline. He learns to control those emotions, thoughts, feelings, and actions which he knows to be abnormal, but has not the power to resist, and thus are prevented those diseases which are largely due to lack of control over the powers which constitute mind and character. Whatever form of psychotherapy is used, whether hypnotism or psychoanalysis, they are incomplete without the process of re-education to healthy reactions and readaptation of the individual to his environment. It is sometimes objected that this can be done without the induction of hypnosis. So it can; but with the class of patients that come to the hypnotist it has already been tried and has failed. Of course, as I have said, not every case of nervous or other disorder treated by hypnosis is cured; nor do I suggest that every such case treated in orthodox fashion should receive this form of treatment. A large number of cases treated by drugs and other acknowledged methods recover. But the hypnotist is not usually consulted until ordinary measures have been given a fair trial, and *it is well to remember that when all other methods have failed there is still a possibility of effecting a cure.*

I have also shown that hypnotism can be used to exercise a great moralizing power. It is not claimed that a real degenerate or genuine criminal can be turned into a law-abiding citizen; but I do assert that if there is any latent good in the man, it can be discovered in hypnosis and made an active guiding principle, a stimulating motive to good conduct. Many people can do that for themselves when they drift into some undesirable habit; but there are others who cannot do so, the habit having got too strong for them, and these require the assistance of one skilled in psychotherapy to draw out the good elements in their character and bring about moral reform.

Hypnotism is not only a valuable therapeutic method, but by hypnotic treatment can be secured accentuated powers of attention, concentration, reproductive memory, and creative faculty; dull minds can be roused to activity, unbalanced minds adjusted, and gifted minds made to develop their dormant talents. Hypnosis is a state in which all the mental faculties can be exalted to an extraordinary degree, bringing out undeveloped capacities and making those already manifested capable of accomplishing greater things than was possible for them before. Where there is a natural gift, often brilliant ideas manifest themselves and the subject works with greater skill in his particular pursuit, as if by intuition, because his subconscious mental activities, of which he was ignorant or which he did not know how to use, are made available to him.

The supernormal capacities which become developed in hypnosis will help to explain the mysterious phenomena of thought-transference, prevision, and clairvoyance on a natural basis. In case those unacquainted with the supernormal phenomena of hypnosis should believe that they may be attributed to credulity or self-deception, I would once more affirm that all the cases quoted have been witnessed by qualified medical men.

The records and explanations given in this volume should convince the reader that hypnosis has a wide range of application, and that there are states of mind, possible forces and influences, which, though at present imperfectly known, may yet eventually be comprehended when hypnotism is regarded as a subject worthy of specific scientific research. To achieve this end is the purpose of this book.

INDEX

Absent-mindedness, 59, 60, 124
ADLER, 92
Advertisements, Suggestion in, 22
Agoraphobia, Treatment of, 90, 91
ALFIERI, 131
Anæsthesia in ecstatics, 126
  in hypnosis, 90, 135
Animal magnetism, 59, 69, 136
Apparitions, *160–164*
ARIOSTO, 131
Art, Suggestive power of, 20
Association of ideas, 39, 45
Asthma relieved in hypnosis, 87
Aura, Human, *137–146*
Automatic writing, 166
Auto-suggestion, 26, 28
  Methods of, *29–33*

BABINSKI, 135, 136
BECHTEREV, 26
BECQUEREL, 139
BERGSON, 103
BERNHEIM, 59, 149
BINET, 112, 135
BJERRE, 78
BLONDLOT, 139
Bodily and Mental Disorders, Treatment of, *82–98*
  Functions, Mental Influence on, 48, 57, 62
Body, Brain Control of, 47, 65
BOSE, 144, 145

Bourru, 110
Braid, 59, 105, 106, 112, 120, 121, 139
Brain, Mental Functions of, 46
Brain-centres, Stimulation of, 110
Brain-control of bodily organs, 47, 65
Bramwell, 117, 135
Brémaud, 103
Breuer, 174
Bué, 137
Burot, 110
Business, Suggestion in, 21

Cazzamali, 144
Challender, 112
Character and Suggestion, 25
Charcot, 126, 134, 171
Charpentier, 139
Children, Suggestibility of, 26
Chorea, Treatment of, 84
Christian Scientists, 81
Clairvoyance, *147–153*
Claustrophobia, 90
Coleridge, 41, 131
Common Sense, 38
Concentration of attention, 45, 52, 68, 69, 75, 79, 123, 125, 126, 129
Consciousness, 36, 38
" Corpse Lights," 141
Coué, 30
Criminal suggestions, 170
Crowds, Suggestibility of, 24
Crystal gazing, 58

D'Abundo, 103
Delboeuf, 118, 126

DICKENS, 128, 130
Disease, Physical treatment of, 80, 81
 Psychical factor in, 80
Dissociation, 37, 60, 61
Drama, Suggestive power of, 21
Dreams and the hypnotic state, *53–55*, 131
Drink and Drug Habits, Treatment of, 76, 92, 93, 168
DRZEWIECKI, 139
DUBOR, 122

Ear-noises, Treatment of, 87
Ecstasy, 59, 126, 130
Ecstatics, 60, 125
EKRIPSY, 143
ELLIOT, 65
ELLIOTSON, 90, 112, 148
Emanations, Human, *137–146*
Emotions, Measurement of, 143
 and Hypnosis, 32, 38, 57, 65, 76, 79, 111, 120, 121, 128, 177
 and Nervous System, 48
Epilepsy, Treatment of, 87
ESDAILE, 90
"Evil Eye," 145
Exaltation of intellectual abilities, *115–151*, 179
Experimental hypnosis, *99–114*

Faith healing, 34, 56
FARNY, 139
FÉRÉ, 112, 135, 142
FOREL, 53, 126
FOTHERBY, 142
FREUD, 61, 92, 174, 175

GASSNER, 56
Genius and self-hypnosis, 89, 127, 128, *129–131*

GOETHE, 131
GRASENBERGER, 106
GREATRAKES, 56
GREGORY, 112, 154
GURNEY, 139

HAENEL, 108
Hallucinations, 41, 60, 156, 157
HASCHEK, 108
Headache, Treatment of, 84
Hearing, Increased power of, 105
HEIDENHAIN, 112
Hereditary dispositions, 25, 29, 37
HERZFELD, 108
HOFFMAN, 131
HOHENLOHE, ABBOT PRINCE OF, 56
HUDSON, 163
Human Emanations, 112, 132, *134–146*, 156, 162
HUMBOLDT, 137
Hypnosis, Accentuation of senses in, *99–114*, *117–119*
  Anæsthesia induced in, 90, 135
  Concentration in, 75
  Conditions of, 74
  Dreams and, *53–55*, 131
  Effect of magnet in, *132–136*
  Emotions in, 32, 38, 57, 65, 76 79, 111, 120, 121, 128, 177
  Experimental, *99–114*
  Explanation of, *50–64*
  Expression of emotions in, 111, 120, 121
  Heightened sensibility in, *132–146*
  Hysterical manifestations in, 171
  Increased intellectual abilities in, 110, *115–131*, 179
  Insanity and, 74, 75, 171

Hypnosis—*Continued*
Methods of, 51, *65–81*
Mimicry in, 120, 121
Moral education in, 18, 26, 97, 178
Organic disease and, 86
Physiological effects in, 82
Public exhibitions of, 58, 71, 167
Reasoning power in, 55
Re-education in, *77–79*, 92, 96, 174, 178
Revival of memory in, 31, 39, 41, 49, 51, 55, 96, 115, 116
Sleep and, *50–53*, 67, 73
Suggestibility in, *56–59*
Suggestion theory of, 56, 59, 149
Surgical operations in, 90
Tests of, 72
Will power in, 15, 168, 169, 172
Hypnotic treatment, Individualization in, 66, 168, 175
Objections to, 15, 61, 73, 99, *167–180*
Relapses after, *172–174*
Summary of claims for, *176–180*
Hysteria, Treatment of, 94

Illness, Suggestibility in, 28, 33
Incontinence, Treatment of, 87
Indirect suggestion, 17
Individualization in hypnotic treatment, 66, 168, 175
Insanity, Treatment of, 74, 75, 95
following hypnosis, 171
Insomnia, Treatment of, 82, 84, 88, 89
Inspiration, 40, 123, 124, 126, 128, 129
Intellectual abilities, Exaltation of, 110, *115–131*, 179

Jendrassik, 126
Joire, 141, 142
Jung, 142

KILNER, 145
"King's Touch," 56, 137
KLEIST, 130
KLOPSTOCK, 131
KRAFFT-EBING, 126

LA FONTAINE, 131
LAMARTINE, 131
LATEAU, LOUISE, 126
LAVATER, 145
LEWES, 128
LIÉBAULT, 126, 137
Lourdes, 34, 56, 84
Love and self-hypnosis, 18
LUYS, 110, 135, 136

McDOUGALL, 61
MAGDELEINE, MLLE, 121
Magnet, Effects of, *132–136*
Magnetism, 107, 108
  Animal, 59, 69, 136
Mahatmas, 125
MARINI, 126
MAYO, 148
Medicines in sealed tubes, Application of, 110
Memory, Revival of, 31, 39, 41, 49, 51, 55, 96, 115, 116
Mental abstraction, 59, 60, 124
  complexes, 77
  discipline, 31, 40, 68, 79, 129, 174, 177
  dissociation, 60, 61
  functions of the brain, 46
  healing, Factors necessary for, 79
  influences on bodily functions, 48, 57, 62
  qualities, accentuation of, 110, *115–131*, 179
  training, 44, 96

MESMER, 59, 108, 171
Mesmeric methods, *69–73*, 137, 150
Mesmerism and Mesmerists, 90, 109, 112, 135, 137, 147, 149, 150, 159
Methods of auto-suggestion, *29–33*
of inducing hypnosis, 51, *65–81*
Mimicry in hypnosis, 120, 121
Mind, Bodily influences on, 48
MOLL, 101, 106, 109, 135, 136, 137
Moral education, 18, 26, 97, 178
perverts, Treatment of, 98
Morbid fears, Treatment of, 90
MOZART, 131
MÜLLER, 139
Muscular tremors, Treatment of, 84, 85
Music, Suggestive power of, 20
Musical ability, exaltation of, 119, 120
Musicians, Inspirations of, 131

Nancy method, 70
Nervous System, Physiology of, 47
and bodily organs, 63
NEUMANN, THERESE, 125
Neuralgia, Treatment of, 84
NEWTON, 131

OBERSTEINER, 136
Objections to hypnotic treatment, 15, 61, 73, 99, *167–180*
Obsessions, Treatment of, 95
Occupational Cramps, Treatment of, 87
ODIARDI, 143
Organic disease and hypnosis, 88
OVIDEO, 130

Pain, Treatment of, 80, 83, 89, 136
Painters, Inspiration of, 130

Paracelsus, 56
Personal Magnetism, 34
Peterson, 142
Physical treatment not to be neglected, 80, 81
Physiological effects in hypnosis, 82
Pitres, 112
Poetry, Suggestive power of, 20
Poets, Inspiration of, 130, 131
Poireault, 139
Politics and Suggestion, 22
Post-hypnotic suggestion, 76
Premonitions, 164, 165
Psycho-analysis, 61, 92, *174–176*

Rays, Human, 112, 132, *134–146*, 156, 162
Re-education, Treatment by, *77–79*, 92, 96, 174, 178
Reichenbach, 134, 140, 141
Reil, 137
Relapses after hypnotic treatment, *172–174*
Ricard, 116
Richet, 158
Richter, 131
Rostan, 138
Russ, 144, 145

Sausse, 136
Savary, 143
Schopenhauer, 128
Scientists and suggestibility, 16
Seckendorf, 131
Self-consciousness, 36
Self-hypnosis, 16, 34, 89, 91, 127, 128, 166
    Love and, 18
    and creative ability, *129–131*
Senses, Accentuation of, *99–114*

Sensibility heightened in hypnosis, *132–146*
Sex-perversion, Treatment of, 92, 93
SIDIS, 112, 135
Sight, Exaltation of sense of, *100–104*
SILVA, 112
Sleep and hypnosis, *50–53*, 67, 73
Smell, Increased sense of, 105
SOCRATES, 130
SOMMER, 108
Stage fright, Treatment of, 31
Stuttering and stammering, Treatment of, 86
Subconscious mind, 26, 29, 30, *36–49*, 54, 60, 62, 63, 126, 129, 130, 159, 168, 169, 177, 179
Suggestibility, Universal, *16–35*
in hypnosis, *56–59*
in illness, 28, 33
of children, 26
of crowds, 24
of scientists, 16
Suggestion, Definition of, 26
Indirect, 17
Methods of, *29–33*, 51, *65–81*
Post-hypnotic, 76
Power of, 134, 135, 136
and heredity, 25, 29, 37
and morality, 18, 26
in business, 21
in politics, 22
Suggestion-theory of hypnosis, 56, 59, 149
Suggestions, Criminal, 170
Suggestive power of advertisements, 22
of art, 20
of drama, 21
of music, 20
of poetry, 20

Supernormal phenomena, *146–166*, 179
Surgical operations in hypnosis, 90

Talents, Stimulation of latent, 122
Tamburini, 135
Tarchanoff, 142
Tasso, 130, 131
Taste, Increased sense of, 108
Telepathy, 146, *154–161*
Temperature, Appreciation of, 108, 138, 139
Thought-transference, 146, *154–161*
Time sense, Increased, *117–119*
Touch, Increased sense of, 107
Treatment by re-education, *77–79*, 92, 96, 174, 178
of bodily and mental disorders, *82–98*
of chorea, 84
of drink and drug habits, 76, 92, 93, 168
of ear-noises, 87
of headache, 84
of hysteria, 94
of incontinence, 87
of insanity, 82, 95
of insomnia, 82, 84, 88, 89
of loss of memory, 96
of moral perverts, 98
of morbid fears, 90
of neuralgia, 84
of obsessions, 95
of occupational cramps, 87
of pain, 80, 83, 89, 136
of perverse sex practices, 92, 93
of spasmodic asthma, 87
of spasms and tremors, 84, 85, 87
of stage fright, 31
of stuttering and stammering, 86

Universal suggestibility, *16–35*

VOLTAIRE, 131

WAGNER, 138
Water diviners, 108
Will power in hypnosis, 15, 168, 169, 172

YELLOWLEES, 101

GEORGE ALLEN & UNWIN LTD.
London: 40 Museum Street, W.C.1
Cape Town: 73 St. George's Street
Sydney, N.S.W.: Wynyard Square
Wellington, N.Z.: 4 Willis Street